CORPUS PALLADIANUM

VOLUME V

CENTRO INTERNAZIONALE DI STUDI DI ARCHITETTURA
" ANDREA PALLADIO "

CORPUS PALLADIANUM

Editor of the Series: RENATO CEVESE

Assistant Editor: ABELARDO CAPPELLETTI

THE VILLA EMO

Giampaolo Bordignon Favero

THE VILLA EMO
AT FANZOLO

Translated by Douglas Lewis

CORPUS PALLADIANUM

VOLUME V

THE PENNSYLVANIA STATE UNIVERSITY PRESS

UNIVERSITY PARK & LONDON

*THE CENTRO INTERNAZIONALE DI STUDI DI ARCHITETTURA "ANDREA PAL-
LADIO" EXPRESSES ITS WARM THANKS TO COUNT LORENZO AND COUNTESS
BARBARA EMO FOR MAKING POSSIBLE THE STUDY OF THEIR VILLA AT FAN-
ZOLO IN CONNECTION WITH THE PUBLICATION OF THE PRESENT MONOGRAPH.*

I SHOULD LIKE TO THANK THE CENTRO INTERNAZIONALE DI STUDI DI ARCHI-
TETTURA "ANDREA PALLADIO" AND ITS PRESIDENT, RODOLFO PALLUCCHINI;
THE CINI FOUNDATION; ERIK FORSSMAN; WOLFGANG LOTZ; AND RUDOLF
WITTKOWER FOR VALUABLE SUGGESTIONS. MARIO ZOCCONI AND ANDRZEJ
PERESWIET SOŁTAN PROVIDED ESSENTIAL MATERIAL, WALPERTO DEGLI AZ-
ZONI HELPED ME LOCATE ARCHIVAL DATA RELATIVE TO WATERCOURSES IN
THE COUNTRY AROUND FANZOLO, AND FRANCA ZAVA BOCCAZZI GAVE HER
GENEROUS HELP. I EXTEND PARTICULARLY GRATEFUL THANKS TO RENATO
CEVESE FOR HIS VALUABLE, KIND, AND PRODUCTIVE ASSISTANCE DURING
THE COURSE OF MY WORK.

G. B. F.

CONTENTS

THE VILLA EMO AT FANZOLO

a - Villa Emo: general view of the south façade

THE ARCHITECTURE OF THE VILLA EMO

THE PATRON: LEONARDO EMO

The interest in the *terraferma* around the middle of the sixteenth century is certainly among the most important aspects of Venetian politics during the Cinquecento, but in connection with this political and economic phenomenon one cannot ignore other aspects of the Venetian world of the time, such as its culture (understood in the broadest sense of the term, with all its artistic implications), Venice's diplomatic activities, its relations with the Holy See, its reactions to heresies, and so on. The interest in the mainland had already been vividly aroused a century earlier, when Venetian nobles had bought farms in the territories of Treviso and Castelfranco, whose annexation on the part of the Serenissima had taken place in 1450. Thus a peaceful penetration, calculated and subtle, had preceded a more massive territorial acquisition; the country sojourns of the patricians became the prologue to a military and political conquest.

Into the area of his rural retreats, the patrician introduced his literary and philosophic "civilization." A refined and cultivated example of this culture is the villa of Marcantonio and Daniele Barbaro in the Asolano. But we must also remember many settlements of Venetian nobles that were determined not so much—or not simply—by humanistic motivations, but rather by practical necessities, and that were destined to affect the economic fortunes of the landholdings and the conditions of their inhabitants. Such is the case with the presence of the Emo at Fanzolo.

We know that even before 1535 the Venetian patrician Leonardo Emo had bought the estate of Fanzolo, composed of 80 Trevisan *campi*, from Andrea Barbarigo. After an intense public activity spent in the service of the state,[1] Emo had decided to initiate concretely the new policy of penetration into the Venetian hinterland. Thus he dedicated himself to the countryside, to land reclamation, to the renovation of agriculture, and to the establishment of grain and spinning mills at Fanzolo, in the territory of Castelfranco. In 1536, by ducal decree of Andrea Gritti, he had already obtained the concession and grant of the "seriola" Barbariga, the watercourse issuing from the irrigation canal of the Brentella (figs. II-III), which—although originally intended for the nearby community of Godego—would water his lands and sustain his animals, since the neighboring townsmen had failed to prosecute their purchase of it.

The entrance of Leonardo Emo into the lands of Fanzolo brought concrete improvements; even though these were perhaps not as extensive as had been anticipated, his presence among the peasants must nevertheless have produced tangible benefits.

He attempted especially to grow Indian corn, known as *granoturco*, which with its fragrant and appetizing *polenta* (or cornbread) replaced the dough of millet locally called "red sorghum" (the "broomstraw" plant used for making hearth-brooms), whose ground kernels had afforded a poor and insipid food. This must have happened quickly, perhaps as an experiment: a proof of the new cultivation is found in a detail of the painted garlands in the Stanza di Ercole and Stanza di Venere, in an intercolumniation beside the door in the southern walls of these rooms leading to the chambers of grotesques, where a sheaf of white cornstalks is represented, with the ears still wrapped in their husks. The presence of the Emo must therefore have been joyfully received by the humblest ranks of the population, accustomed to protracted shortages and to hunger; indeed, Leonardo accomplished a crucial change in the standards of the peasants by introducing an amelioration of their daily fare.[2]

The site which he had chosen at Fanzolo corresponded to his agricultural requirements (plates 1-3). It lay on a vast plain spread out between the Brenta and the Piave, with the distant semicircle of Alpine foothills forming toward the north an open crown above the land. Moreover, there was an abundant water supply from the time of his acquisition of the estate: the canal of the Brentella, which extended to this point, was not yet systematically channeled but dispersed itself in numerous rivulets that were diverted by one or another of the local landholders (figs. II-III).[3] Leonardo accommodated the situation to his own plan by requesting (and definitively obtaining) the canalization of the diverted "seriola" for his use. Thus his program was actually accomplished in full, if a fact which must have appeared in the process of planting the new crops did not

frustrate some of his plans: the naturally alluvial site proved somewhat arid and was correspondingly less productive because of its permeability.

It was natural that Leonardo should want to live on these lands that he had tended and loved and that he should build a new dwelling in place of that of the Barbarigo. Demolishing the ruins of the latter for the construction of his villa (plates 4-6, 8-10; scale drawing *a*), he engaged the most distinguished architect then working in the Veneto: Andrea Palladio. This must have taken place between the date of his grant in 1536 and 1559, the year in which he died.[4] It is highly probable that the villa had been completed—at least in its structural parts—before 1559, or at any rate that its beginning dates from about 1555.

We do not know what arrangements were made between Palladio and Leonardo Emo about the villa at Fanzolo. The contracts and original designs have neither been found on the site nor at Padua in the archive of the Palazzo Emo Capodilista, where the family's documentary holdings are preserved. Even so, we must suppose that Leonardo knew Palladio primarily through his many civic and military administrative and managerial posts. It would not be absurd to maintain that an encounter between the patrician and the artist might have taken place while the former was governor of the province of Friuli—that is, at the time of his administration in Udine—even though not a single document exists to support this possibility. We know only that in 1556, three years before Leonardo's death, Domenico Bollani had the entrance gate to the *castello* of Udine built as a memorial to the city's liberation from a famine and plague. It has been suggested that in April of 1556 Palladio also went to Udine to begin the construction of a palace for Floriano An-

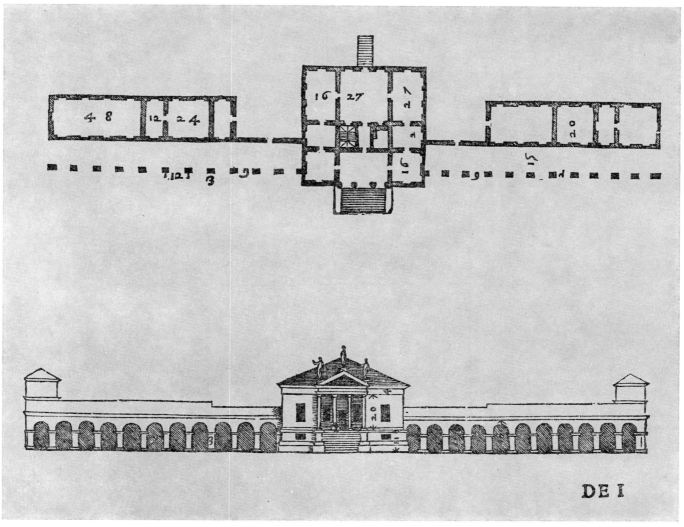

I - Andrea Palladio, *Plan and elevation of the Villa Emo at Fanzolo.* From *I Quattro Libri dell'Architettura*, Venice, 1570, II, XIIII, 55

tonini and (perhaps contemporaneously) the black marble access portal to the Sala d'Ajace in the municipal hall of the same city.[5] Nothing further can be added to the argument, beyond the simple citation of a probable connection between works in Udine.

A possible incentive toward villa-building may have come to Leonardo Emo as early as 1509 when he was living in Padua, where Falconetto's buildings were already appearing. Falconetto was influenced by the teachings of Alvise Cornaro, enemy of theorists but friend of artists, who was a member of Bembo's circle, a builder of houses, an agriculturist, and land-reclaimer.[6] Cornaro also wrote architectural treatises,

not for gain through their sale "but to teach and inspire the citizens to build," since he knew that from the understanding of architecture was born "the delight and pleasure of spending"; this had happened to him, for no sooner had he begun to appreciate the pleasures of building than he had been induced to spend beyond his means on it.[7] And it is also necessary to recall that close to Fanzolo, at Treville di Castelfranco, Michele Sanmicheli had already built "... il famosissimo palagio dei Soranzi, dalla detta famiglia detto 'la Soranza', ... tenuto per abitura di villa, il più bello e il più comodo che insino allora fosse stato fatto in quelle parti. ..."[8]

Perhaps during this period a smaller

villa was erected as well, at Sant'Andrea oltre il Muson near Castelfranco, also in the vicinity of Fanzolo: it was commissioned by the Corner family and was subsequently frescoed by Benedetto Caliari.[9] Certainly Leonardo had seen the imposing palace of the Soranzos, already completed by 1551,[10] and perhaps also the smaller villa a short distance away. At the same time, in Piombino—again not far distant from Fanzolo—Giorgio Corner, called Zorzon, erected a villa different from Leonardo's on a plan by Palladio. If this villa was the "habitation" indicated by Giorgio Corner in a document of 1556,[11] we would have almost an absolute certainty that it had been seen by Leonardo Emo, and one would be led to suppose that he was stimulated by it to begin his own villa on the lands at Fanzolo.

At Fanzolo there seem to be indications everywhere of the personality of the patron, who must have prescribed for his own dwelling a country house that should be an exemplary agricultural center and granary (plates 4-6, 8, 22-27, 29-33; color plate a). The project probably obtained its source of income from cattle-raising, a speciality in the restricted economy of Fanzolo. In the decoration of his house, as well, Leonard Emo perhaps wished to give pride of place to figures of classical mythology, ancient history, and religion, to those of allegory and symbolism, with allusions to domestic and popular virtues—such as the necessity for irrigation, or the social rapport between patrons and peasants essential to the increased productivity of the land.[12]

Leonardo's versatility is manifest: *provveditore della Repubblica* (one must emphasize the significance of his former office), he was the coordinator of the site with its watercourses, the setting with the new villa, the architecture and the decoration, and of the whole decorative ensemble. The coordination of single elements must have been the result of a predetermined intent, answering to a clear and communicable ideal based on the many requirements of cultivating the fields and caring for the animals, as well as all the other purposes which must be considered in the renewal of a socio-economic organism. The most diverse social strata of the time, even those formerly opposed to each other—landowners or nobles, peasants and clergy (the latter cultivated by the Republic during this period through fear of the Protestants, the Anabaptists, and the Turks)—were thus able to initiate a reciprocally fruitful dialogue.

The design of the villa in the "Quattro Libri"

Ten years before the construction of the Villa Emo, as Vasari notes, the celebrated palace called "La Soranza" was built for the Soranzo family at Treville di Castelfranco Veneto, the work of Michele Sanmicheli.[13] Palladio must have seen Sanmicheli's building, given the fame which it enjoyed; and perhaps at least a vague reminiscence of La Soranza is evident in the Villa Emo (fig. I; plates 1-4; scale drawing f), in its similar horizontal alignment of buildings, in their connections, and in the prominence of the central block in relation to the rest of the structures.[14]

La Soranza was composed of three elements: the dwelling block and two dependencies. Two lateral pavilions also projected forward from the ends of the central part, thus emphasizing its volumetric quality. The single-storied wings were each fronted by an arcade of eleven bays (as at the Villa Emo) and were given over to agricultural functions.

We do not mean to affirm here that Sanmicheli's work should be seen as a

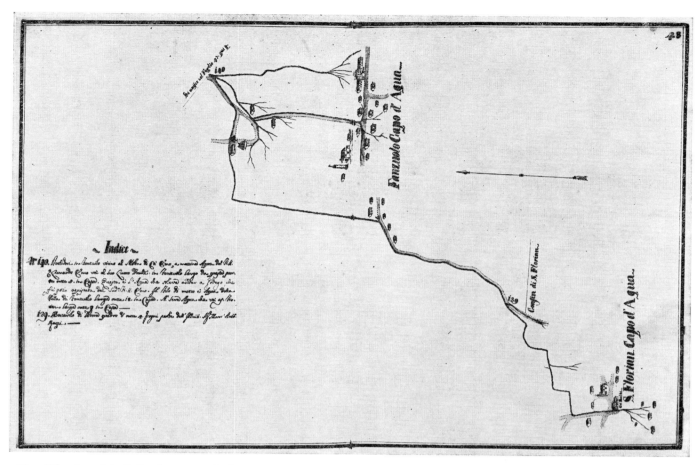

II - *The " seriola " Barbariga and the Villa Emo at Fanzolo.* From *Dissegno generale di tutta la Brentella*, 1763

determining antecedent to Palladio's conception for Villa Emo, but rather simply to note the presence in the territory of Castelfranco of a building of enormous architectural importance, which was among the first and most conspicuous Cinquecento dwellings of the Venetian patriciate on the mainland.

Palladio was sixty-two years old when *I Quattro Libri dell'Architettura*, already anticipated for some time in the circle of his admirers, appeared in 1570.[15] We know that by 1556, the period in which Daniele Barbaro published *I Dieci libri dell'architettura di Vitruvio*, Palladio had prepared the greater part of the first draft of his treatise (within exactly what limits, however, is not known), which was destined to appear only fourteen years later. On this point Barbaro's testimony[16] is precise and demonstrable.

In the 1570 Venetian edition of De' Franceschi,[17] Palladio published the design of the Villa Emo in Fanzolo (fig. I), describing it simply and sparely, reduced to its essentials: " ... Le Cantine, i Granari, le Stalle, e gli altri luoghi di Villa sono dall'una, e l'altra parte della casa dominicale, e nell'estremità loro vi sono due colombare, che apportano utile al padrone, & ornamento al luogo, e per tutto si può andare al coperto: ... Dietro à questa fabrica è un giardino quadro di ottanta campi Trivigiani: per mezo il quale corre un fiumicello, che rende il sito molto bello, e dilettevole. È stata ornata di pitture da M. Battista Venetiano." [18] For an exact understanding of the work, one must refer to the general considerations contained in the chapters on the "Decoro, o convenienza, che si deve osservar nelle fabriche private," the "Compartimento delle stanze, & d'altri luoghi," the "Atrio di quattro colonne," the "Sito da eleggersi per le fabriche di Villa," and the "Compartimento delle case di Villa." [19] It is opportune to recall as well the passages relative to porticoes,[20] since in the Villa Emo these constitute the means by which "per tutto si può andare al coperto" (plates 2-6, 8, 22-26; scale drawings *b-f*): "... I coperti per le cose di Villa si faranno havendo rispetto alle entrate, & à gli animali, & in modo congiunti alla casa del padrone, che in ogni luogo si possa andare al coperto: acciò che nè le piogge, nè gli ardenti Soli della State li siano di noia nell'andare à vedere i negotij suoi: il che sarà anco di grandissima utilità per riporre al coperto legnami, & infinite altre cose della Villa, che si guasterebbono per le pioggie, e per il Sole: oltra che questi portici apportano molto ornamento."

Notwithstanding a few alterations, the villa as executed is, all in all, substantially faithful to the design of 1570 (fig. I; plate 4; color plate *a*; scale drawing *f*), not only in form but also in its measurements (see Appendix I).

THE PLAN

The numbers one reads on the plan in the treatise (fig. I) indicate clearly the number of "feet" which the rooms were to measure, in both length and width. From the design, we see that the central hall is a square of 27 feet (the Vicentine foot corresponds to 34.75 cm., and thus 27 feet equal 9.38 meters); that the two rooms adjacent to it, as well as the loggia, form rectangles of 27 by 16 feet (9.38 m. by 5.56 m.); and that the two rooms on the south are 16-foot squares (5.56 m. by 5.56 m.). The depth of the porticoes in the wings is also given (15 ft., or 5.21 m.), as well as the size of the openings of every arch in the dependencies (9 ft., or 3.12 m.) and of the thickness of each of their piers (3 ft. by 2 ft., or 1.04 m. by 69.5 cm.).

The distribution of spaces in the buildings of the two wings, or "barchesse," is interesting: they show no symmetrical correspondence between the two parts, because their arrangements reflect the stipulations of the "compartimento delle case" in terms of the appropriate "allogamento" of men or beasts, of "granari, cantine, o tegge." [21] But in their present form, the result of transformations effected in the eighteenth century, the eastern wing is adapted as part of the owner's section, while the western wing, which also incorporates the chapel, contains rooms again reserved for the needs of the proprietors (see the scale drawings, which record the present state of the building).

The main stair affording access to the loggia appears in the plan as divided into equal steps 5.56 m. long (a measure not indicated, however, by Palladio), but this does not correspond to the actual situation (plates 2-4, 9-10; scale drawing *c*). The plan also shows a small flight on the rear façade, sharing the same axis as the principal stair; it is no longer extant, but was recorded by Bertotti (fig. IV). Alterations carried out two centuries ago replaced it with two small diverging flights (scale drawings *b-c, g-i, k-l*) that descend from a narrow landing.

The passage from the front garden to the rear is masked on the Palladian plan by a curtain wall which establishes the connection of the two wings to the central block; but the wings appear detached by an interval of 36 feet (12.51 m.), a span equivalent to three bays of the dependencies [22] (see Appendix I). The separation indicated on the Palladian project is in reality (scale drawings *b-g, l*) reduced so as to correspond to the width of one

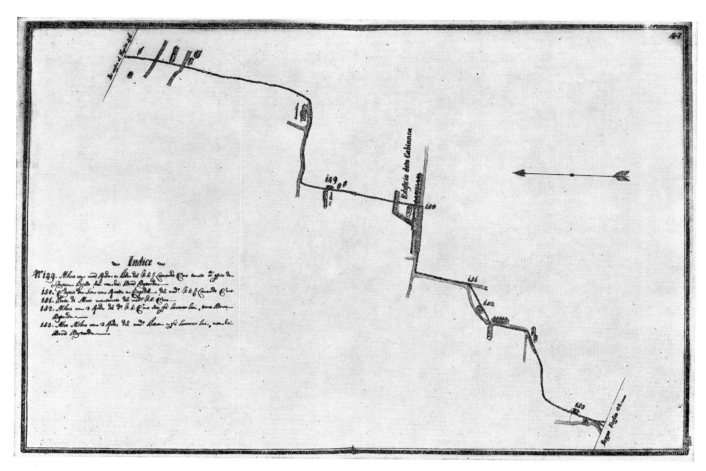

III - *Leonardo Emo's farms and mills along the " seriola" Barbariga in Fanzolo.*
From *Dissegno generale di tutta la Brentella, 1763*

bay, and the rear wall of the portico is now closed, apart from a small door recently cut through it.

THE ELEVATION

The rendering of the elevation is correlated with that of the plan, as far as the principal block is concerned. Palladio indicates its vertical dimensions, limiting them to the basement (11 ft., or 3.82 m.), to one of the columns of the loggia (from the base to the capital, 20 ft., or 6.95 m.), and to the terminal cornice (4 ft., or 1.39 m.). Also, he clearly furnishes the measurements for the elevation of the porticoes: the height of an arch at 18 feet (6.25 m.), the width of a pier at 3 feet (1.04 m.).

The main stair giving access to the loggia repeats the division into equal steps. An indication of the high podia enclosing the stair is included as well.

The design shows in addition three acroterial statues of considerable height on the angles of the pediment, but not the two tiny windows of the attic (opened, in the execution of the project, in symmetrical correspondence to those in the basement), the tympanum sculpture, or two other square windows above the rectangular ones in the loggia. The absence of these latter windows further demonstrates the summary character of the design. Their correspondences with those in the central hall and with Zelotti's decorations, which are virtually contemporary with the fabric, ensure their authenticity (plates 11-12,

35); evidently they were necessary either for practical reasons or for compositional balance.

Another incongruity between the elevation and the plan on Palladio's plate is seen in the break in level of the roofs between the eastern and western dependencies; on the elevation the break corresponds to the width of four bays on the right (equivalent to 48 ft., or 16.68 m.), while on the plan (and on the left of the elevation) it corresponds to three bays (equivalent to 36 ft., or 12.51 m.).

THE HARMONIC MEAN PROPORTIONALS

The measures of the Villa Emo furnished in Palladio's treatise, reconsidered recently by Wittkower,[23] pair off as the obvious responses to architectural laws based on the principles of humanism, which had established a fundamental rule elaborated by nearly all the most accomplished architects of the time. The rule laid down by Leon Battista Alberti was successively validated, after their considerations of Vitruvius, by Daniele Barbaro and Palladio himself, who were linked to Trissino's circle of Neoplatonists and to Vicentine Aristotelians (but opposed, in part, by the Paduan intimates of Bembo, with Alvise Cornaro's distrust of precedent). This rule encouraged a transferral of the ratios of musical harmonies into the proportions of architecture, in all its constituent elements and in all the relationships of these elements with the whole body of a building. Palladio actually dealt with the subject explicitly in his *Quattro Libri* in the section " Dell'altezze delle stanze," [24] and he had previously become acquainted in particular with the theories of the harmonic mean proportionals formulated by Padre Francesco Giorgi, from whom Doge Andrea Gritti had commissioned a report

(1525) following the disagreements over Sansovino's design for the Venetian church of S. Francesco della Vigna.[25]

On the subject of the harmonic proportions of the Villa Emo, Wittkower comments that " a thorough acquaintance with Renaissance ideas on proportion is often necessary to understand the legitimacy of the ratios given by Palladio. In the Villa Emo rooms of 16 x 16, 12 x 16, 16 x 27 frame the portico (also 16 x 27) and the hall (27 x 27). The ratio 16 : 27 can only be understood by splitting it up in the way Alberti has taught us; it has to be read as 16 : 24 : 27, i.e. as a fifth and a major tone (= 2 : 3 and 8 : 9) and similarly the compound ratio 12 : 27 can be generated from 12 : 24 : 27, i.e. an octave and a major tone (= 1 : 2 and 8 : 9). Thus the figures 27, 12, 16 which, written one under the other, strike the reader's eye, are perfectly intelligible by means of the generation of ratios. Ratios of the same order are to be found in the wings; 12 is again the middle term, this time inscribed between 24 and 48. The harmonic character of this series is obvious (2 : 1 : 4, 1 : 4 being two octaves = 1 : 2 : 4). The whole building appears now like a spatial orchestration of the consonant terms 12, 16, 24, 27, 48." [26]

In the light of the above observations on the Palladian design of the Villa Emo (and on its inconsistencies), the publication of the treatise can be held [27] as being subsequent to the realization of the project. In fact, the publication must have constituted for the architect a kind of ideal presentation of his work, with indications of things that he had not done as fully as he would have been able to do had he not encountered obstacles to their execution. The book, therefore, was not an " itinerarium mentis " of the master, but a practical " excursus," perhaps even a cursory one, with the primary intention of

b - G. B. ZELOTTI: *Prudence* and *Abundance* (above the entrance arch to the central hall)

ennobling the works already executed and in part also of modifying them to meet the needs of future patrons.

Thus, if the fragment of 1561 already contains a description of the Villa Emo in Fanzolo, together with others, then this provides yet another consideration in support of the chronology proposed above, that by the year of Leonardo Emo's death in 1559 the building may have been entirely completed, if not yet altogether finished in its decorative program.

THE STRUCTURAL REALIZATION

At the Villa Emo the elements are co-ordinated according to a paratactical disposition rather than following a subordination by syntactic dependence, giving an almost urban stamp to the building complex: its elements are all "separate but equal." In fact, the spaces also are co-ordinated and distinct; the dwelling block is equally distinct with respect to the wings,[28] and in a certain sense these seem from the elevation to be distinguished from the almost autonomous dovecotes (plates 1-4, 23, 25-27; scale drawings *f, g*).

ORGANIZATION OF DWELLING SPACES

Palladio, guided by the symmetry of the Roman baths, affirmed that the ancients never neglected symmetrical correspondences. Such a declaration, Wittkower writes, even though expressed in a particular context by the master, can still be found exemplified in the architecture of the villas. Wittkower, presenting in a diagram the schematized plans of eleven Palladian villas—among which that of the Emo at Fanzolo appears as the most simplified of all—gives a geometrical compendium of the spatial structure of all the villas.[29]

In addition to the disposition and correlation of the spatial units (scale drawing *d*), it should be noted that a rhythmic alternation of heights occurs as a fundamental and characteristic factor throughout the architecture of the Villa Emo. The entrance loggia is thus succeeded by a narrow vestibule, sharply reduced in width and about half as high as the preceding space, which leads into the hall (scale drawing *i*). From the latter, whose vertical development is identical to the loggia's, one proceeds into the noticeably lower rooms on the north and thence to those on the south (of the same height as the northern rooms). One passes between them through two small chambers of grotesques (scale drawing *j*), once more reduced in height, which thus appear as secondary areas of communication. Between the southern rooms and the high loggia the height of the spaces alternates as in a cyclical cadence.[30]

Seen in regard to the internal spaces, the façade acts as their introduction. In studying the relationship between the front and the interior, one has almost the sensation that the villa has no vertical lift (scale drawing *d*; plates 4, 9-10), since the basement is so insignificant compared with the ramp: it seems almost as if the central block descends to the level of the ground or of the wings, or even that these and the ground are raised to the level of the upper landing at the foot of the colonnade. The smaller windows placed above and below the windows of the main floor indicate the modulation of heights in the concatenation of interior spaces.

The loggia, with its columns, windows, and tympanum sculpture (scale drawing *f*; plates 4, 10), corresponds to the central hall, with its portals and windows (plates 45-46) and its carved arms of the Emo

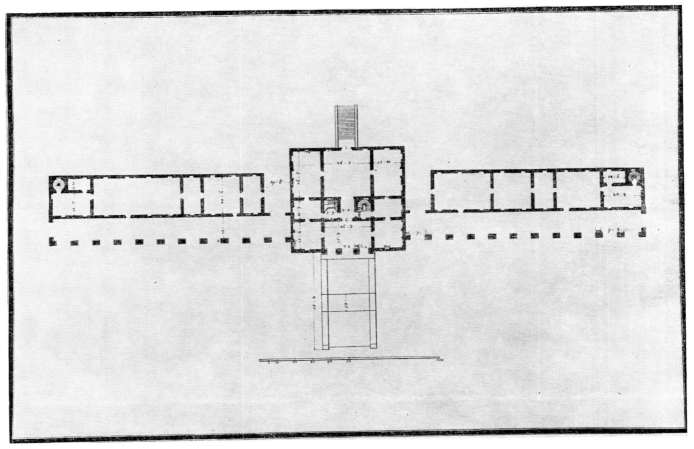

IV - Ottavio Bertotti Scamozzi, *Plan of the main floor of the Villa Emo at Fanzolo.*
From *Le Fabbriche e i Disegni di Andrea Palladio*, Vicenza, 1781, III, pl. XVIII

family. A window in front corresponds to the rooms flanking the central hall, and the contrast on the façade between the rising pediment and the base line of the terminal cornice corresponds to the diversity in height of the ceilings within (plates 10, 15-16).

Because of its wings, the villa seems to be projecting itself into the surrounding countryside (plates 1-6, 22-23, 25, 29-31), and its central block, prolonged by the broad access stairs and a vast marble pavement, appears to mark the middle of an ideal axis, which is continued to the north and south by long avenues of poplars (plate 1; scale drawing *a*). Thus the dwelling block is the point of encounter of two matrices: one architectural, formed by the open structures of the dependencies, and the other natural, constituted by the great arboreal avenues.

As we approach the villa, it seems as if the principal block advances (plates 4, 9-10), while by contrast the extremities of the wings appear to recede through the effect of the dovecotes, which are set on structures behind instead of providing a façade termination for the arcades (scale drawings *e-f, l*; plates 2-6, 8, 23, 25-27). The portico does not project but is recessed into the dwelling block, so that its columns are aligned with the adjacent walls (plates 4-11, 16). The triangular pediment does not noticeably raise the line of the roof; although limited in height (scale drawing *f*; plates 4, 9), it is still sufficient to contain an heraldic shield supported by two great winged Victories (plate 15), the single decorative gesture on the exterior of the extremely simple fabric.

Simple in the portion reserved for the owner, the structure is even simpler in the

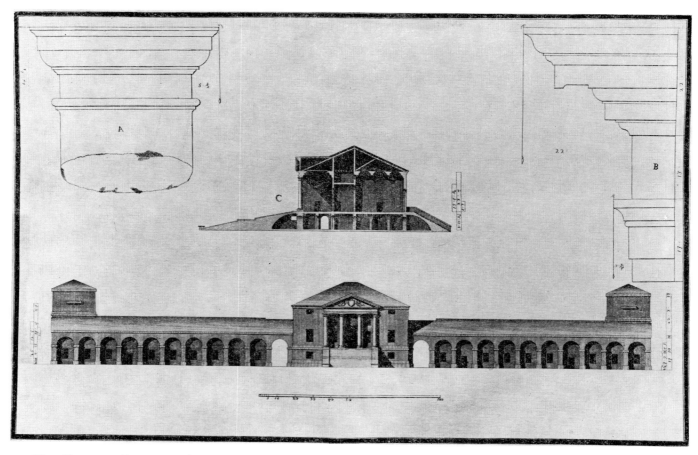

V - OTTAVIO BERTOTTI SCAMOZZI, *Façade elevation and transverse section of the Villa Emo at Fanzolo.*
From *Le Fabbriche e i Disegni di Andrea Palladio*, Vicenza, 1781, III, pl. XIX

arcades, where the arches are placed on piers with capitals reduced to an unmolded strip (scale drawings *f, l*; plates 22-28). Even the podia of the access stair (which is contemporary with the villa and not later, as has repeatedly been maintained [31]) are expressed as simple oblique surfaces (plates 9-10) that follow the incline of the marble ramp with a minimum projection in height (scale drawings *c, i, l*).

THE VILLA EMO COMPARED TO THE VILLA BARBARO AT MASER

The type of villa which Palladio created at Fanzolo balances that which he built for Daniele Barbaro at Maser: a prominent central block flanked by two wings or dependencies, with the towered dovecotes providing a symmetrical conclusion to the whole edifice. But the near-identity of the architectonic concepts—which, however, were inspired by two clearly diverse environmental situations—did not prevent Palladio from resorting to expressive forms which had little in common.

The Villa Emo is opened to the surrounding atmosphere by its three high Tuscan intercolumniations; Villa Barbaro is closed, its wall articulated only by the four Ionic shafts which form its vigorous ligature. The sculptural decoration in Villa Emo is peremptorily restrained within the triangular perimeter of the pediment (plates 10, 15); at Villa Barbaro it breaks its bounds, falling across the arch of the window of the main floor, where it rather unexpectedly interrupts the trabeation of the order. Here the master took advantage of an expressive freedom unquestionably suggested by the problematical style of

Mannerism. The windows in the Villa Emo lack cornices (plates 7, 9; scale drawing *f*) and appear as dark spots on the unbroken smoothness of the walls; at Maser they are provided with quite elaborate frames.

At Fanzolo the dependencies extend in undifferentiated sequences as far as the two dovecotes, which, although set back, still form an idealized terminus; at Maser the rhythmic progression of the arcuated wings is interrupted by the two enormous lateral units, where complex and elaborate architectural facings—another example of Mannerist taste—mask the simple towers of the dovecotes. The decoration at Maser is profuse throughout, from the squared niches of the arcades to the keystones of the arches, the lavish tympanum of the principal block, and the nymphaeum. The spare, essential language of Villa Emo—which eschews the slightest concession to extra-architectonic factors—reveals the artist's intellectual vigor: his *poesia* wells up, limpid and pure.

Comparing the plans (scale drawing *c*), that of the Villa Emo could not be simpler, formed as it is of three fundamental and parallel axes: the principal one is constituted by the loggia and hall, linked by the narrow vestibule; the two minor ones, which are perfectly equal and symmetrical, are made up of spaces that share a common measure (the width of the northern and southern corner rooms and the length of the chambers of grotesques). Conversely, the plan of Maser is much more complex, especially since the principal block is composed of two sectors: one which forms part of the elongated horizontal body and subsumes its central spaces, and another which is detached from it and extends toward the lower slope of the hill. In a certain sense the latter sector acquires a planimetric articulation of its own, so that it becomes the rather short longitudinal bar

of a cross whose transverse bar is considerably longer.

The spatial units at Fanzolo are blocked out in rigidly prismatic shells (plates 45, 49, 59, 68, 73, 75, 78, 110, 114; scale drawings *i-j*) that have beamed ceilings—except for the vestibule, which has a barrel vault (plates 43-44, 47-48), and the basement rooms under the main block (plates 19-21; scale drawing *j*); the spaces of Maser are defined as extremely elastic shells, covered with ceilings which are sometimes barrel-vaulted and sometimes groined. Still, the central hall at Fanzolo, with its rich, compartmented ceiling (plates 45-49, 51, 59; scale drawing *i*; see pp. 41-42), is one of Palladio's most harmonious spaces, and it is appropriate to underline its exceptional beauty.

Beside Fanzolo and Maser, Palladio's production does not include any other villas of such open compositional layout: the treatise, in fact, indicates some totally closed forms (e. g., the Villa Pisani at Bagnolo, the Villa Thiene in Quinto Vicentino, and the Villa Sarego of Santa Sophia) and others in which the dependencies, after leaving the main block, turn at right angles to enclose three sides of a large courtyard, thus generating a rectangular form which is lacking one of its long sides (e. g., the villas Pojana at Pojana Maggiore, Saraceno at Finale di Agugliaro, Zeno at Cessalto, Ragona at Ghizzole, Repeta at Campiglia, Angarano at Angarano, and Godi at Lonedo). Similar to the latter type are the villas Badoer at Fratta Polesine, Trissino at Meledo, and Thiene at Cicogna, even though their arcades are curved into quadrants.

By its total openness to the atmosphere through its long dependencies and by its immersion in the space of the surrounding countryside, the Villa Emo becomes one of Palladio's most inviting and friendly expressions: at the same time simple and solemn, the suggestive evocation of a classical image, it is also extraordinarily contemporary in the everyday life of those working and producing, with the labor of their arms and the dedication of their minds, within its setting.

The Villa Emo
and the rural building tradition

The elements which make up the architecture of the Villa Emo, separately considered, derive from local rural building traditions. That is, they represent the elements of an antique architecture which, firmly implanted with the Augustan division into hundreds (whose boundaries and architectural expressions still constitute the most obvious and permanent images in the farmlands of the Veneto), survived through an exarchal reorganization as a reduced dialect of the Late Imperial language. Rural habitations maintained their forms across centuries, if not millennia, without calling attention to the innovations brought about by later developments.

The residential part of the Villa Emo is the very simple, geometric nuclear element of a peasant dwelling, if we exclude the temple-front. Even the ramp belongs to a remote rural heritage, as a simple, inclined plane that was favored for communication with the proprietor's house precisely because of its lack of steps. Along it one could roll casks or drag bundles, provisions, and furnishings; on it grain could be spread out to dry in the sun (as occurs even today) or the kernels of wheat more quickly separated from the chaff, in an expanse which reached from the columns across the paved courtyard floor as far as the entrance gate to the villa.

Above the living floor lay the attic, which again was rustic in its evident function as a granary, with two tiny rectangular windows immediately under the slope of the roof. The wings or dependencies, with their elemental forms made up of prismatic piers supporting on each side eleven semicircular arches, are themselves simplified structures, and the two turrets or dovecotes, almost hidden behind the wings at their ends, derive as well from standard rural building practice. All maps of the *terraferma* and all drawings of buildings on rural estates depict such structures, which have the same appearance and the same proportions as the two at Villa Emo. They belong to the type of towers on a square plan and are likewise subdivided into levels corresponding to the cells for the pigeons.

The stucco decoration and
woodcarving of the Vittorian school

Almost corresponding to the tympanum sculptures on the façade (plates 10, 15) is another great Emo coat of arms (plates 44-45) located in the hall, above the large door giving onto the lawns at the rear. It is carved in wood, painted, and gilded, set within scrolls and crowned by the Lion of St. Mark, facing toward the right and flanked by two mailed fists holding a sword of justice and a staff of command with a crested helm. One can establish a chronological correlation between this heraldic ornament and Zelotti's decoration from the fact that the pictorial framework was executed specifically to contain the arms, surmounting them with two slender swags of painted cloth whose folds are held by leonine heads.

There can be no doubt that the sculptural decoration of the pediment, as well as the wooden sculpture of the hall, are both reminiscent of Alessandro Vittoria's style. In fact, an analogy is evident, even if the similarity is not exact, when the tympanum of Villa Emo is compared with that of Villa Pisani at Montagnana, executed (according to the researches of Zorzi and Cessi) between 1553 and 1557.[32] The carved arms in the hall—composed of interlaced garlands, animals, and symbols, winged sirens, dolphins, and eagles—recall, in their superabundant ornament and in the "nudi serpentinati" which characterize them, Vittoria's winged creatures in the Villa Garzoni (now Carraretto) at Ponte Casale.[33] But even if the design of the wooden arms and of the external stuccoes is Vittorian, and if the date is within the range indicated above, the execution of the work could still have been carried out by assistants of the master. Among these, if we exclude Bartolomeo Ridolfi—who was so highly regarded by Palladio, according to Vasari, that if he had been the author of these works the architect would surely have recorded it[34]—we might suggest the name of Agostino Ridolfi, Bartolomeo's son, himself an accomplished sculptor, to whom the lessons of the great Vittoria could hardly have been unfamiliar.

NOTES

Works cited in the notes only by the author's surname and date may be found fully described under that date in the Bibliography beginning on page 54.

[1] SERENA, 1929, p. 28.

Already on 3 September 1446 Giovanni di Francesco Barbarigo, a nobleman of the Veneto, had appeared before the Uffizio delle Acque of Treviso to ask permission to channel a " seriola," or watercourse, in the usual way from the large Brentella (sometimes called "Piavesella") canal to his own lands at the villa of Fanzolo (ibid., pp. 29, 124-128; the transfer of the property from the Barbarigo to the Emo is indicated, as well as the demolition of the Villa Barbariga). The documents relative to the Emo's request and the grant of the diversion and use of the " seriola Barbariga," then called " di Godego," are preserved in the archives of the Consorzio Irriguo Brentella di Pederobba at Montebelluna, collated in the " Libro rosso dell'Officio delle Acque di Treviso" of the sixteenth century (see Bibliography), later transcribed in a copy of 1688 at the same archive, under the following entries:

a) Litterae Ducales (Gritti) quibus concessa fuit portio aquae plavisellae renuntiata per Comune et Homines Villae Gutici Clarissimo Domino Leonardo Emo (Venezia, 12 settembre 1535).

b) Litterae Ducales (Gritti) committentes executionem Litterarum suprascriptarum (Venezia, 3 febbraio 1536).

c) Litterae Ducales (Gritti) quibus revocatae fuerunt litterae concessionis aquae clarissimo domino Leonardo Emo et aliae committentes executionem illarum (Venezia, 16 marzo 1536).

d) Concessio aquae Plavesellae facta per collegium aquarum Tarvisii clarissimo domino Leonardo Emo (Treviso, 18 marzo 1536).

e) Litterae Ducales (Gritti) Laudantes concessionem ut supra factam per collegium aquarum Tarvisii clarissimo domino Leonardo Emo (Venezia, 25 marzo 1536); and in the " Dissegno generale di tutta la Brentella ...," 1763, fols. 47, 48.

N. H. Leonardo Emo was born in 1473, son of the patrician Giovanni Emo (RUMOR, 1910, pp. 73-76). It is worthwhile to emphasize that this Leonardo Emo is not the one mentioned generally in the Palladian literature (MARCHESAN, 1908, p. 43; BURGER, 1909, pl. 39; RUMOR, 1910, p. 39; LOUKOMSKI, 1927, pp. 87-90; MOLMENTI, 1928, p. 210) as the patron of the villa at Fanzolo but was instead the uncle of that personage. This fact becomes evident for chronological reasons, through the documentation surrounding the acquisition of the lands (as well as the residence) of Fanzolo, because of renovation and the demonstrable use of irrigation, the farming, the demolition of the older owner's dwelling, and the erection of the new villa on the same site.

The elder Leonardo, who married Elena, daughter of Pietro Balbi in 1501 (RUMOR, 1910, p. 74; SERENA, 1929, p. 128, n. 72), was soon given notable appointments by the Signoria. In 1504 he was chosen to bear the general's staff of command to the Conte di Pitigliano in the war against Pope Julius II (ROMANIN, 1913, V, p. 218; SERENA, 1929, p. 128, n. 72). In 1509 he was *provveditore* and companion of the future doge Andrea Gritti in the defense of Padua against the League of Cambrai (RUMOR, 1910, p. 74; SERENA, 1929, p. 128, n. 72), and subsequently he achieved a personal victory at Brescia, which had been blockaded by the French. In 1514, while governor of the *Patria del Friul* at Udine, he negotiated an armistice with the imperial troops, who had already penetrated to the shore of the Lagoon and taken Marano del Friuli (ANTONINI, 1873, p. 203; ROMANIN, 1913, V, p. 295). During the following year (1515), still at Udine in the same governorship, he restored the Cappella della

Madonna, erected in the Church of S. Maria delle Grazie dei Servi by his father, to whom he dedicated a marble bust (RUMOR, 1910, p. 75).

In 1520 he was *podestà* at Verona (ANTONINI, 1873, p. 213), and in 1523 he was urgently called to Milan as a counselor of war on the occasion of a rapid incursion of the French (ROMANIN, 1913, V, p. 386). In 1526 he ingeniously proposed to the Senate a new type of ordnance for arming the Venetian galleys (*Venezia e le sue lagune*, 1847, I, 2°, p. 171). And from 1535 onward, after such an extensive public service, he did not simply withdraw into his own occupations, but concretely planned —if he did not directly initiate—the new politics of penetration into the Venetian hinterland.

He died in 1559 and was buried at Venice in San Nicola dei Tolentini, in the family tomb, where his descendants dedicated to him the following inscription: " Patricio Viro Leonardo Hemo non minus animi quam corporis et fortunae bonis praedito, qui post administratam rem publicam, multis numeribus et domi et foris fortissime peractis grandaevus aetatis concessit..." (RUMOR, 1910, p. 76).

[2] The corn, or *granoturco*, came from Spain, imported in turn from Mexico and Peru (i.e., from the pre-Columbian cultures). In exchange, the Spaniards brought wheat to America. D. BELTRAMI, *Saggio di storia dell'agricoltura nella Repubblica di Venezia durante l'età moderna*, Venice, 1955, pp. 11, 21, notes that according to Ramusio, Indian corn was already cultivated in the territories of the Polesine and Rovigo and in the southern part of the province of Verona around Villabona; in 1582 it began to be used in Venice for blended grain, and between the end of the sixteenth and the early seventeenth century it was planted in various localities of the Trevisano.

We know that the lands of the Polesine were then largely owned by the Emo; thus Ramusio's passage may also reflect Leonardo's efforts in Fanzolo, at least as a trial or experiment for the Trevisano.

[3] SERENA, 1907, p. 31.

[4] RUMOR, 1910, p. 76; SERENA, 1929, p. 128 (n. 72).

[5] The date of 1556 for the palace of Floriano Antonini at Udine was noted by G. G. Zorzi as appearing on a medal, on one side of which appeared a portrait of Count Antonini and on the other the supposed image of the palace. This date was followed by other writers (PANE), but R. MARINI, in " Il Palazzo Antonini " (MS at the Centro Internazionale di Studi di Architettura "A. Palladio" [noted hereafter as " C.I.S.A."] in Vicenza), maintains that the beginning of the palace dates from the years 1550-52. Marini's supposition, which is supported by strong arguments, would completely deflate the tradition of Palladio's going to the capital of Friuli for the commission of this palace. The date of the Bollani arch is legible in the inscription. T. TEMANZA, *Le vite de' più celebri architetti e scultori veneziani del sec. XVI*, Venice, 1778, pp. 297-298; G. G. ZORZI, "Andrea Palladio in Friuli," in *Archivio Veneto Tridentino*, V, 1924, pp. 124, 127-128; PANE, 1961, p. 24.

[6] G. BORDIGNON FAVERO, *La Villa Soranza di Michele Sanmicheli a Castelfranco Veneto*, Treviso, 1958, p. 25.

E. FORSSMAN, " Falconetto e Palladio," in *Bollettino del C.I.S.A.*, VIII, pt. 2, 1966, pp. 52 ff.

[7] G. FIOCCO, " Alvise Cornaro e i suoi trattati di architettura," in *Atti dell'Accademia Nazionale dei Lincei. Memorie, Scienze Morali, ...*, ser. 8ª, IV, iii, 1952.

We should not fail to mention, concerning this undertaking by Leonardo Emo, the reflection of an ambience which is not widely known and which was antithetic to the theoretical mentality of the Paduan school; this was the one afforded by the Arsenale di Venezia. It was mentioned earlier how Leonardo Emo by 1526 had given suggestions for the ballistics of new ordnance which he proposed to the Senate for the armament of the Venetian galleys. The Arsenale was an extraordinarily novel environment, teeming with scientific life and experiment; it was unreceptive to the Aristotelians and Averroists and was a point of encounter for discussions and for talents opposed to doctrinaire conclusions. In this unusual and experimental ambience of the middle of the sixteenth century, we can imagine Leonardo Emo and Andrea Palladio as attentive observers of the novelties of that "natura che non istupidisce, ma che alimenti i sensi."

[8] G. VASARI, *Le vite de' più eccellenti Architetti, Pittori, et Scultori ...*, Florence, 1550, "Vita di Michele Sanmicheli."

[9] MAZZOTTI, 1954, pp. 543-544; BORDIGNON FAVERO, *op. cit.*, 1958, p. 48; G. MARIACHER, "La Villa Corner-Chiminelli di Castelfranco Veneto," in *Acropoli*, 1960-61, fasc. iii, pp. 173 ff.; L. CROSATO, *Gli affreschi nelle ville venete del Cinquecento*, Treviso, 1962, pp. 184-186.

[10] BORDIGNON FAVERO, *op. cit.*, 1958; P. GAZZOLA, *Michele Sanmicheli, architetto veronese*, Venice, 1960, pp. 153-154.

[11] "Archivio dei X Savi sopra le Decime di Rialto," 1566; no. 664, Museo Correr, Venice. PALLADIO, 1570, II, p. 53.

[12] Here one must defer the interpretation of certain decorations (in the loggia, in the chambers of grotesques, and in a lunette in the Stanza delle Arti) because of their socio-religious allusions to ancient practices of agrarian cults and of sorcery, widely revived in the middle of the sixteenth century in the Veneto (C. BERNARDI, *Asolo*, Milan, 1949, pt. 1, p. 51) and perhaps also in Emilia, as well as in Friuli. Cf. W. WOLTERS, "Andrea Palladio e la decorazione dei suoi edifici," in *Bollettino del C.I.S.A.*, X, 1968, pp. 255-267.

[13] VASARI, *op. cit.*, 1550, "Vita di Michele Sanmicheli."

[14] E. LANGENSKIÖLD, *Michele Sanmicheli—the Architect of Verona*, Uppsala, 1938, p. 36.

[15] PANE, 1961, p. 81.

[16] D. BARBARO, *I Dieci libri dell'architettura di M. Vitruvio tradotti e commentati...*, Venice, 1556, VI, p. 179: "... Io mi estenderei in discrivere particolarmente molte cose ... ma sapendo che presto venirà in luce un libro delle cose private, composto et dissegnato dal Palladio ... non ho voluto pigliare la fatica d'altri per mia. ..."

We know that, in fact, the *Quattro Libri* of 1570 had had a fragmentary previous draft, which is now preserved at the Museo Civico Correr in Venice. These fragments, according to Zorzi—who studied them with particular care—"include a general and a specialized section of the treatise. Of the first, general part there exist the fragments of two distinct and successive compilations; the first made between 1561 and 1565, the other begun in 1565 and, in any case, preceding the definitive printed edition of the treatise. The specialized part, including the descriptions of several palaces and villas, all belongs to the first compilation and was repeated in its entirety (with minor corrections) in the published treatise of 1570. An examination of the handwritings shows that all the fragments (except for some short marginal notes in Palladio's own hand) are the work solely of Silla Palladio, youngest son of the architect, who largely transcribed in a handsome copy an autograph manuscript of his father, following the latter's style and way of thinking. ..."

Comparing the description "delle case di Villa di alcuni Gentil'huomini di Terra Ferma" contained in the Correr fragment with the same part in the treatise, "it can be seen that the order and wording are the same. Only in the case of two villas is there a slight variation, specifically for the Palazzo Pisani at Montagnana ... and the Villa Emo at Fanzolo, at the end of the description of which Palladio himself has added the words, '...è stata ornata di pitture da messer Battista Venetiano [Zelotti],' which were then repeated in the treatise." Cf. FORSSMAN, *op. cit.*, 1966, pp. 52 ff.

[17] PALLADIO, 1570, II, xiiii, p. 55.

[18] Ibid.

[19] These passages, cited from Book II, refer respectively to chapter i, p. 3; ii, p. 3; v, p. 27; xii, p. 45; xiii, p. 46. Cf. E. FORSSMAN, *Palladios Lehrgebäude*, Stockholm, Göteborg, Uppsala, 1965, pp. 52, 65, 75. BIEGANSKI, 1968, p. 23.

[20] PALLADIO, 1570, II, p. 46.

[21] Ibid.

[22] PANE, 1961, p. 228, n. 11.

[23] WITTKOWER, 1965, pp. 131, 134.

[24] PALLADIO, 1570, I, xxiii, p. 53.

[25] F. GIORGI, *De harmonia totius mundi*, Venice, 1525. (The memorandum on Sansovino's church design was published by G. MOSCHINI, *Guida per la Città di Venezia*, 1815, I, i, pp. 55-61, reprinted in WITTKOWER, 1964, pp. 151 ff., and translated in WITTKOWER, 1965, pp. 155-157, repeating previous English editions of 1949, 1952, and 1962.) WITTKOWER, 1965, pp. 102-107.

[26] WITTKOWER, 1965, pp. 130-131.

[27] ZORZI, 1955, pp. 95 ff., n. 4; WITTKOWER, 1965, p. 21, n. 2.

[28] ZEVI, 1966, cols. 67 ff. Cf. P. BIEGANSKI, "I problemi della composizione spaziale delle ville palladiane," in *Bollettino del C.I.S.A.*, VII, pt. 2, 1965, pp. 28-29.

[29] WITTKOWER, 1965, p. 73. SALMI, 1963, p. 491, judges artificial the classification of Palladio's numerous villas into "villa-temples," for those of a single order (Badoer at Fratta Polesine, Emo at Fanzolo, etc.), and "villa-palaces," for those of superimposed orders (Pisani at Montagnana and Corner at Piombino).

[30] PALLADIO, 1570, I, p. 52.

[31] The drawings executed by the C.I.S.A. have demonstrated that the ramp is original. Indeed, it would not have been possible to construct a stairway, given the fact that in proximity to the loggia the greater angle and depth of the steps could not have accommodated the curvature of the basement vault, which presently extends under the topmost landing of the ramp—at least not unless Palladio had intended a rather wide landing as an ideal prolongation of the pavement of the loggia, perhaps at a level one step lower. However, this is highly improbable from other points of view.

[32] ZORZI, 1955, pp. 95 ff. F. CESSI, *Alessandro Vittoria—architetto e stuccatore*, Trent, 1961, pp. 28 ff. Cf. A. BLUNT, "I rapporti tra la decorazione degli edifici del Veneto e quella della scuola di Fontainebleau," in *Bollettino del C.I.S.A.*, X, 1968, pp. 153-163.

[33] CESSI, *Alessandro Vittoria—bronzista*, Trent, 1960, p. 45; dated 1562.

To these carved arms we can relate other works of the master, such as the Lion of St. Mark on the balcony of the Palazzo Ducale facing the Piazzetta, the monument to Girolamo Grimani in San Giuseppe di Castello at Venice, and the plaque in the Palazzo Ducale commemorating the Venetian visit of Henry III of France (CESSI, *op. cit.*, 1961, pp. 107, 109, 112).

[34] ZORZI, 1955, pp. 95 ff.

c - G. B. ZELOTTI: *The Death of Virginia* (eastern side of the central hall)

APPENDIX I

GRAPHIC RENDERINGS OF THE VILLA EMO

The first edition of Bertotti Scamozzi [1] dedicates two plates with ample commentaries to the Villa Emo (figs. IV-V). Bertotti's design appears notably more elaborate than Palladio's: the architectural scale is indicated to a length of 100 feet, divided into tens in its first half (i.e., from 0 to 50 ft.); in turn, the first half of the first ten (i.e., from the beginning of the scale to the fifth foot) is subdivided in inches. This rendering is therefore more detailed and useful for measuring the building than the summary one in Palladio's treatise; but it is not precise, since there are more than a few differences between the measures which it furnishes and those of the building as executed.

The access stair to the loggia appears on Bertotti's plan as it stands today (not simply 16 Palladian feet long, but rather 55 ft., 2 in.), composed of two ramps broken in the middle by a ten-foot landing.[2] The two ramps, gently inclined and of a majestic amplitude, seem less like a stair than a grandiose pavement directly linking the loggia to the court and the surrounding countryside.

The rear staircase—which is coaxial with the ramp on the entrance front [3]—survives, beyond a portal 6 feet (2.08 m.) wide, or of the same dimension as that affording entrance from the loggia.

The interval between the principal block and the two wings already appears reduced to about one third in respect to the Palladian plan. Bertotti opens the connecting curtain wall only behind the first arch of the dependencies, in line with their piers (fig. V). In this regard, we may refer to one of Bertotti's observations on the plates, intended to clarify the exigencies governing the distribution of the parts of the villa: "La forma della sua Pianta è un quadrato, e le adiacenze che la fiancheggiano sono di una significante lunghezza in proporzione della Fabbrica principale ... ."

With respect to Palladio's design, one also notes a different distribution of internal spaces in the two wings, almost as if their apparent shift toward the central block had afforded the possibility to express at the ends of the *barchesse* the structures [4] of the two towers or dovecotes, which had appeared in the 1570 design only on the elevation and not in the plan. Evidently, either the eighteenth-century restorations have modified the Palladian plan, or there were departures during the execution from the design as published in the treatise. Indeed, since Palladio indicated the elevation of the dovecotes, it seems strange that he did not show on the plan the corresponding rooms with their stairs.

Another interesting indication on Bertotti's plan is the particular location of the two small stairs within the principal structure, connecting its *piano nobile* with the ground floor and with the loft in the attic. These stairs, illuminated by apertures in the loggia which are shown in its elevation, occupy about half the area of the spaces in which they stand; the other half serves as a corridor to connect the chambers of grotesques with the vestibule, whereas on the Palladian plan the staircase west of the vestibule takes up that whole space. Here again we see an indication of the summary character of Palladio's design.

An argument for the original existence of these structures as Bertotti shows them is the presence of a door opening symmetrically from each chamber of grotesques into the service area containing the stairs. This door opened in the dividing wall is, in fact, perfectly consonant with the decorations of the *grottesche*, whose arrangement has not been altered at all; indeed, Zelotti took the situation into account in painting his architectural and perspectival illusions.

Another careful rendering of Bertotti's plan is that showing the columns of the loggia, whose bases turn out actually to be supported on square plinths. The central intercolumniation is wider by one foot than the two side ones, whose widths are equal. In consideration of the loggia, Bertotti adds: " La proporzione di questa Loggia è di una larghezza e 2/3, che si avvicina a una terza maggiore, cioè a quella proporzione che passa fra il 3. e il 5.; e la sua altezza è determinata colla media proporzionale Aritmetica."

Thus, in the same effort to discover harmonic proportions, the rooms flanking the loggia are considered as nearly square, while the rectangular ones have a length equivalent to their width augmented by two-thirds, which—as in the above-mentioned passage—" corresponds to a major third."

The dimensions of the windows in the owner's dwelling are measured as well, and those of the four corner rooms (3 ft., 4 1/2 in. = 1.30 m.) prove wider than those of the central hall (3 ft. = 1.04 m.). The presence of a fireplace is also indicated in the corner rooms.[5]

In close relation to the plan stands the elevation in plate XIX (fig. V). The design of the ramp is here apparent; it is not flanked by the usual Palladian podia but is accompanied in its gradual slope by a slightly raised section which almost imperceptibly defines its width.

Behind the colonnade the windows are clearly indicated by black shadings, as are the unmoulded upper windows, neither of which appear on the Palladian design. Similarly evident are the two little windows within a hair's-breadth of the upper cornice, which act as counterpoints to those in the basement of the fabric. In addition, the arches attaching the wings to the central block appear open, with a correspondent lowering of the ridgepole of the roof.

Within the pediment of the villa, Bertotti indicates the decoration with the painted arms of the Emo family, which is not shown in the plate of 1570.

In the rendering of the elevation (fig. V), the measurements indicated at the edges of the plate specify the various levels. Thus one finds at the right the height of the socle supporting the piers (which corresponds to that on which the ground floor of the owner's dwelling is placed, and which constitutes the linking external element for the whole building), the height of the piers themselves and of their capitals (formed by a fascia which becomes the first cornice of the central fabric), and the height to the apex of the arches. Bertotti also specifies the following heights: that of the wings as far as the eaves; the cornice strip beneath them; and that of the dovecotes to their crowning cornice. In the left-hand measurements one finds the levels of several apertures: a window in the basement, one in the central block, and that of the entrance portal of the loggia.

Confronted with the stylistic problem of the portico, and of its colonnade in particular, Bertotti found himself perplexed, since his mentality was unable to comprehend a definition and classification outside the catechisms of the Enlightenment. Neither the proportions, nor the division of the parts, nor their shape—in short, nothing about them—approached the measures and forms with which Palladio was (or seemed to be) accustomed to endow his Doric-inspired buildings. Bertotti could not define the character of the architectural order of the loggia, although it is evidently Doric, since the columns were too high for the Doric proportion and

their capitals, although patently corresponding to those of the order, differed from its orthodox forms. Thus it turns out that the ensemble has proportions which are neither Doric, Tuscan, nor Ionic. Consequently Bertotti wanted to call it "Composite," or a Doric of which a capable hand could doubtless have varied the parts.[6]

On the same plate as the elevation is depicted a section through the central block of the villa, flanked by two details giving the capital of a column and a profile of the entablature of the order. The section reconfirms many elements already noted in the plan and elevation: the front ramp and rear stair appear nobly arranged so that each seems necessary to the other, both as an equilibrium of weights and in their function as "embankments" to sustain the building. The attic loft is shown directly above the vestibule linking the loggia with the hall; close to a corner of the vestibule a door is visible, leading to the service area with the interior stairs and from thence into the chambers of grotesques. The original arrangement of the coffered wooden compartments in the hall ceiling is also shown; Bertotti, however, declares them to be "... presentemente coperti con una volta leggera di una piccola porzione di cerchio." Meanwhile the profile of the roof appears for the first time, with its trusses and the raised section—looking like a large dormer—of the pedimented temple-front.[7]

We may note as well the existence of a closed space under the ramp, which has only one small aperture for light; the present arrangement differs substantially, although it seems quite unlikely that this should postdate Bertotti's designs. Today there is a corridor (plate 19) extending the full width of the villa to link the two wings. From this gallery one gains access to the service areas (the winecellar, the owner's storerooms, and the kitchen), which are located beneath the central block.

At the right of Bertotti's section are three columns of measurements, which indicate, respectively, the height of the vestibule on the *piano nobile*; the height of the ground floor, above which is placed that of the loggia and the hall; and, finally, that of the doors on the main floor.

In showing the profiles of the capital and the entablature, drawn on the same plate, Bertotti gives their respective measures. For the capital, the height from the "cimacio" to the "collarino" is noted, inclusively and also individually for the "collarino"; for the entablature, the height of the architrave and frieze and—in a single measurement—of the components of the cornice: the cyma reversa, the fascia, the corona, and the cyma recta.

Regarding the idea of harmonies on the elevation, Bertotti attempts a disquisition similar to that which was noted for the plan, but his observations on the subject are hardly enlightening. The results are either inaccurate, through defect or excess, or invalidated by over-optimistic opinions.

In his conclusion, however, Bertotti gives a detailed encomium of the order, the beauty, the elegance, the proportional correctness, and the exemplary character of this villa; values which "... dovrebbero insegnare agli architetti che è ben permesso di scartare qualche volta i precetti dei Maestri, purché non si offenda né la ragione, né il buon senso e che non si esca dai limiti che sono stabiliti."

EIGHTEENTH-CENTURY MODIFICATIONS

During the eighteenth-century adaptation of the wings, a domestic chapel with ornaments of paneling and stuccoes was arranged in the western part. Its chancel section is raised, with a crossing dome. The illumination derives from a glazed lunette over the entrance door. On the altar is an eighteenth-century painting (signed) by Antonio Marinetti, called " il Chioggiotto."

As a second modification, it should be noted that the ceiling of the hall, though invisible, was still in place at the beginning of the present century, since it had been plastered over and enclosed by a heavy nineteenth-century overpaneling; Marchesan [8] records its sole subject, in which "... si vuole fossero dipinte le Muse." Burger saw it in 1909 in all its completeness, with " an assembly of Olympian divinities and a figure of Jupiter in the center stretched out on the model of Michelangelo's *Night*." Between 1937 and 1940 [9] the Palladian cofferings were restored, in the loggia as well as in the hall, by Mario Botter at the expense of Count Corrado Emo. [10]

MEASUREMENTS OF PLANS AND ELEVATIONS OF THE VILLA

It can be interesting to compare the measures indicated by Palladio with those furnished by Bertotti Scamozzi, and especially with the modern ones drawn up in 1967 for the C.I.S.A. (by the architects Mario Zocconi and Andrzej Pereswiet Sołtan) for the scale drawings in the present volume. The divergence which exists between the modern drawings and those by Bertotti is a significant warning with regard to the inaccuracy of Bertotti's data. We should mention at once that the measures given by Leoni, Ware, and Muttoni (figs. VI, VII, VIII) are taken bodily from the plate in the *Quattro Libri* and consequently will not be considered here. [11] The measurements given by Mucci (fig. IX) correspond to those given by Bertotti.

PLANS: THE CENTRAL BLOCK

Northeast and northwest corner rooms

	length	width
Palladio:	9.38 m.	5.56 m.
Bertotti:	9.23 m.	5.50 m.
C.I.S.A.:	9.44 m.	5.66 m.

Central hall

	length	width
Palladio:	9.38 m.	9.38 m.
Bertotti:	9.23 m.	9.12 m.
C.I.S.A.:	9.45 m.	9.33 m.

Chambers of grotesques

	length	width
Palladio:	5.56 m.	(not given)
Bertotti:	5.50 m.	3.73 m.
C.I.S.A.:	5.60 m.	3.80 m.

Southeast and southwest corner rooms
(These are very nearly square, since the difference between length and width is negligible.)

	north and south walls	east and west walls
Palladio:	5.56 m.	5.56 m.
Bertotti:	5.50 m.	5.38 m.
C.I.S.A.:	5.62 m.	5.62 m.

Combined width of main-floor rooms on east-west axis (width of central block)

Palladio:
excluding thickness of walls 20.50 m.
Bertotti:
excluding thickness of walls 20.12 m.
C.I.S.A.:
excluding thickness of walls 20.66 m.
(including thickness of walls 22.35 m.)

THE DEPENDENCIES

Arches

Palladio:	width 3.12 m.
Bertotti:	width 3.12 m.
C.I.S.A.:	width varies from 3.12 m. to 3.14 m.

Depth of arcades

Palladio:	5.21 m.
Bertotti:	4.51 m.
C.I.S.A.:	4.63 m.

Depth of rooms
Palladio: 6.95 m.
Bertotti: 7.12 m.
C.I.S.A.:   7.40 m.

ELEVATIONS: THE FAÇADE

Vertical dimensions of the central block

Palladio:	basement	3.82 m.
	walls	6.95 m.
	cornice	1.18 m.
—	total height	12.16 m.
Bertotti:	basement	3.76 m.
	walls	6.70 m.
	cornice	1.29 m.
—	total height	11.97 m.
C.I.S.A.:	basement	4.22 m.
	walls	7.36 m.
	cornice	0.61 m.
—	total height	12.19 m.

Total length of the villa, including dependencies
Palladio: 114.95 m.
Bertotti: 113.76 m.
C.I.S.A.:   118.23 m.

Height of dependencies, excluding cornice
Palladio: 6.25 m.
Bertotti: 6.19 m.
C.I.S.A.:   6.29 m.

Height of dovecotes, including cornice
Palladio: (not given)
Bertotti: including cornice: 14.71 m.
C.I.S.A.:   including cornice: 13.81 m.

Height of arches in dependencies
Palladio: 5.21 m.
Bertotti: 5.18 m.
C.I.S.A.:   4.96 m. (from pavement of arcade) [12]

NOTES TO APPENDIX I

[1] BERTOTTI SCAMOZZI, 1781, Book III, pp. 23-25, pls. XVIII-XIX. Also interesting are the plates of Villa Emo which accompany the texts of Leoni (fig. VI), Ware (fig. VII), Muttoni (fig. VIII), and Mucci (fig. IX).

[2] "...che Requie si chiama: acciocchè, deboli e stanchi ritrovino dove posarsi: e intervenendo che alcuna cosa di alto caschi: habbia dove fermarsi ... "; PALLADIO, 1570, I, p. 61; PANE, 1961, p. 28; F. FRANCO, " Ottavio Bertotti Scamozzi," in *Bollettino del C.I.S.A.*, V, 1963, pp. 152-161.

[3] Afterwards pulled down.

[4] Composed of a spiral stair with two adjacent service spaces, forming a complex more than 20 feet square. A. CHASTEL, " Palladio et l'escalier," in *Bollettino del C.I.S.A.*, VII, pt. 2, 1965, pp. 11-22.

[5] The fireplace in the Stanza dell'Amore di Giove ed Io was lined in the seventeenth century with precious blue-and-white tiles from Delft, depicting religious, mythological, and military scenes with figures, animals, etc.—attributed, in fact, to designs by the greatest Dutch masters of the period.

[6] FOPPIANI, 1844, I, iii, p. 36, nn. 26 and 27.

[7] PALLADIO, 1570, I, p. 7.

[8] MARCHESAN, 1908, p. 102, n. 1.

[9] MAZZOTTI, 1954, p. 717.

[10] PANE, 1961, p. 228, n. 11; BRANZI, 1961, p. 34 ff.; MAZZOTTI, 1962, pp. 819-820.

[11] The measures given by Palladio and Bertotti are expressed in Vicentine feet, one of which corresponds to 34.75 cm.

[12] Measuring the height of the arch from the level of the garden, one would be obliged to add the height of two steps (corresponding to approx. 41 cm.) to the 4.96 meters. Thus the total height would be 5.37 meters. It should be noted that Palladio's and Bertotti Scamozzi's plates bear no indications of steps. Those executed have no constant dimensions.

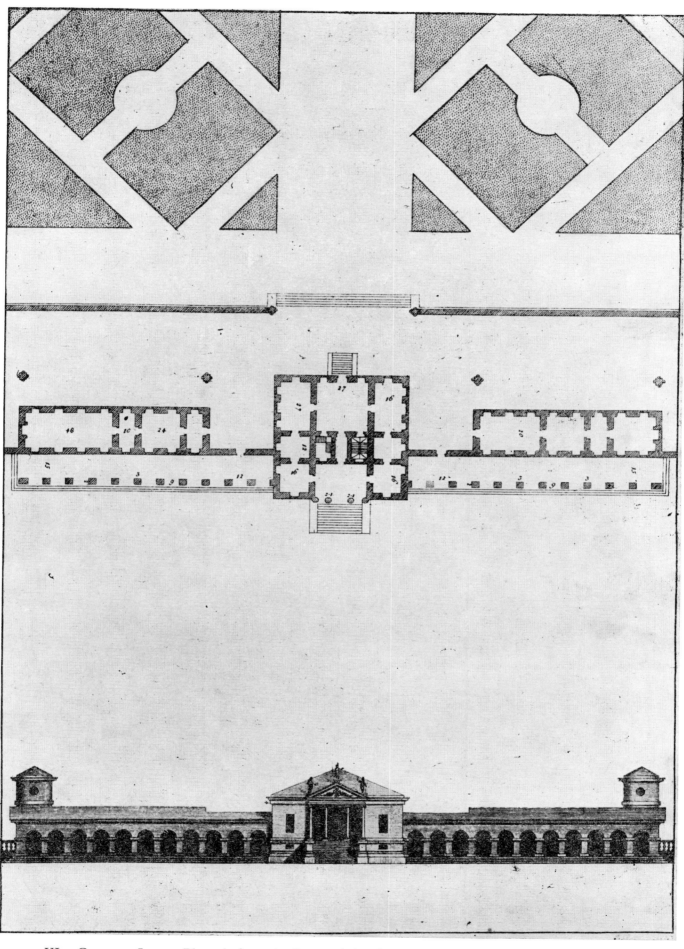

VI - GIACOMO LEONI, *Plan of the main floor and façade elevation of the Villa Emo at Fanzolo.*
From *L'Architecture de Palladio ...*, The Hague, 1726, I, II, pl. XL

THE PICTORIAL DECORATION BY GIOVAN BATTISTA ZELOTTI

Giovan Battista Zelotti, called "Battista Veneziano," was the decorator of the Villa Emo. We can be sure of this, because Palladio affirms it in his treatise [1] and because Zelotti's authorship (after much discussion [2]) has been confirmed on stylistic grounds by the critics most responsible for defining the artist's personality, from von Hadeln to Fiocco and from Crosato to Pallucchini. [3]

In regard to the chronology of the frescoes, the problem which has been of most recent interest to scholars may be considered solved, at least within approximate limits. Since the paintings at Fanzolo are mentioned in the description of Villa Emo in the De' Franceschi edition of Palladio's treatise published in 1570, while the preliminary manuscript of the text, dated between 1561 and 1565, contains an added note in Palladio's own hand (evidently later than the section drafted by his son Silla) specifying that the villa "è stata ornata di pitture da M. Battista Venetiano," it has been concluded that they were probably executed between 1565 and 1570. [4] According to Crosato, an earlier dating to the years around 1560 might be justified by a stylistic definition or equilibrium related to a moment shortly after the cycle of Villa Godi at Lonedo (circa 1557) but not to the rather "derivative" phase of other pictorial complexes around 1570. Thus the latter consideration would advance the date of the frescoes to a point at which the villa must have been just barely finished, virtually in coincidence with the death of its patron in 1559. But

considering Zelotti's many commitments during the years around 1560—when he was working at Brugine, at the Malcontenta, at the Monte di Pietà in Vicenza, and at the Abbey of Praglia—Pallucchini has more aptly proposed that the time-consuming complex at Fanzolo would not have been executed until about 1565. [5]

The achievement at Fanzolo thus stands as a culmination of the finest and most productive period of Zelotti's activity; after his association with Veronese, which was fundamental and decisive in his stylistic orientation, he was arriving at the affirmation of a substantially autonomous manner and a decorative taste of his own.

We have no means of knowing what his youthful work was like in collaboration with Paolo at La Soranza (1551)—in which Zelotti was able to see how his great associate discovered from the art of Sanmicheli the character and the value of architecture as an exalting and clarifying force for his figures [6]—nor can we describe the later association of the two masters in the Vicentine palace of Iseppo da Porto (just after 1552). However, the frescoes by Zelotti accompanying those by Fasolo in the "Camerone" of the Palazzo Porto Colleoni at Thiene, datable to about 1552 [7] (even if they cannot be compared with possible works by Paolo in the same palace, as mentioned by the sources [8]), already reveal in their bold chromatic juxtapositions the stamp of Veronese, which was the primary stylistic component of Zelotti's pictorial taste. In any event, the canvases of 1553 in the hall of the Council of Ten in the

Palazzo Ducale, on which the two painters and Ponchino collaborated, and the central octagon of 1554 in the hall of the *Tre Capi* share in their formal arrangements a robust mannerism Michelangelesque in character, while an emphasis on solutions of Veronesian quality demonstrates Zelotti's power of balancing his expressive means.

The two masters again collaborated on the *tondi* for the Libreria Marciana (1556) and at the Palazzo Trevisan in Murano (1557); but by this time, with his fresco cycle for the Villa Godi at Lonedo,[9] Zelotti had already begun to depart from Veronesian models, dedicating himself independently to the type more congenial to his skill as a decorator. His next works have an inventive novelty deriving from his more personalized style, evident in the ceiling of the Palazzo Chiericati at Vicenza, with the Council of the Gods (1558)[10] flanked by splendid *grisailles*, and in the decorations of the Villa Roberti at Brugine (c. 1560); from Ridolfi's description (1648) we can recognize the importance of other Vicentine frescoes at the Monte di Pietà (1558-63), which were much admired by Vasari but are now lost.

Around 1560, at the Malcontenta, Zelotti achieved a perfect union between the decoration and the Palladian space. Little remains of these paintings, but in the superabundant decoration of the great hall one can still discern the well-organized spacing of his figures. The whole Mannerist repertory of Mantuan derivation is here subordinated, serenely reflecting the architectonic structure. Thus the elements remain what they are, but are arranged according to a new order: the gems are beautiful in their solitude, and the images are situated and enframed by architectonic requirements.

To these examples of Zelotti's production must be added his work at the Abbey of Praglia, which lasted from 1559 to 1564;[11] here the master confronted exclusively sacred imagery for the first time, ably treating these themes not only in the frescoes of the church but also in the canvases set into the library ceiling, where the individual decorative elements are organized within compartmented divisions.

Thus, toward the middle of the 1560s Zelotti approached his full stylistic maturity in the decoration at Fanzolo, which may be considered as a perfect example of his figurative vocabulary. He was exclusively a decorator, whether he dedicated himself to fresco-painting or to his more limited and intermittent work in oils (his canvases often appear harsh and shrill, but they are still suggestive as surfaces of blaring color, supremely decorative within their massive gilded frames), preferring profane subjects but not neglecting sacred ones.

At the Villa Emo the mythological scenes of the rooms recall various experimentations with frescoes in the villas decorated earlier; however, the two historical scenes in the hall could almost be classified as easel-paintings, as in their illustrative and expressive intent they are related to the "hanging" pictures of sacred subjects that seem to be suspended, with their frames, as overdoors in the corner rooms. It should also be possible to trace at Villa Emo the results of Zelotti's work at Praglia,[12] insofar as it seems correct to emphasize a compositional analogy—which also reflects a chronological link—between the decorative frieze of sacred scenes on the drum of the dome of the abbey church and the fictive relief, also continuous, of the lower zone in the villa hall, representing a triumphal procession extending across the whole dado course on both the eastern and western walls. The taste for grotesques also has precedents in those of the Malcontenta,[13] which closely recall certain details as well as the stylistic freedom of the grotesques at Villa Emo: the latter have been almost

d - G. B. Zᴇʟᴏᴛᴛɪ: *Fame* (overdoor on the eastern wall in the Stanza d'Ercole)

overlooked by critics, or else suspected of revealing another hand. Zelotti was an exquisite craftsman of detail, accomplished in the observation and representation of cameos, gems, crystals, and engraved stones, and a nimble executor of portraits, reliefs, histories, and symbols, all abundantly present at Villa Emo, though arranged with calculated discretion.

At Fanzolo Zelotti created a decorative arrangement more finely organized and disciplined than any to be encountered in his later activity, which becomes less unified because of the participation of collaborators, and perhaps less spontaneous; from this the suspicion might arise that Zelotti had followed unusually precise—and largely justified—suggestions from Palladio himself.[14] In fact, it is perfectly credible that the architect might already have conceived a decoration for Villa Emo consonant with the stipulations of Leonardo Emo, who could well have aspired at once to a combination of sacred themes with aristocratic-doctrinal and rustic ones. And it would have been logical that, after having conducted his spectator and guest into the hall by way of a route past the loggia and all the other parts of the great house, he would have wished his proscenia and scenes to have been set off as they are here by the delightful little chambers of grotesques.

THE ARCHITECTURAL DECORATION

Vitruvius had written about the decoration of villas, and the taste for mural paintings within a fictive architectural framework was neither new nor exclusive to Villa Emo. Thus Roman taste, recapitulated in a period more severe than its predecessors, had substituted for the figural apparatus of divinities and mythological cycles a style of wall-painting based on illusionistic architectural elements such as podia, columns, and entablatures. Almost all the sixteenth-century villas in the countryside of the Veneto reflect this scheme of figured architecture, and, in fact, the taste may have spread from Verona, where the first edition of Vitruvius was brought out in 1511 by Fra' Giocondo.[15]

At the Villa Emo the order of the loggia (plates 35, 37-38) recurs in the form of decorated Tuscan columns in the painted responds on the rear wall, and the corner member serves as a support for flanking structures in which the same columns reappear. The lateral intercolumniations are opened by a door, further embellished by a play of recessed and projecting cornice blocks, above which are grouped incidents from the hunt of Diana. Between the shafts of the order (plates 37-38), dangling by violet garlands from the mouths of lions' heads, hang festoons of fruits and flowers.

Around the windows at the back of the loggia (plate 35) the painter has simulated marble frames with triangular pediments and projecting cornices; above these, in the upper zone of the walls, two busts stand out against scalloped niches, from which descend the usual polychromed festoons. Zelotti further animates the solemn entrance wall above the high portal with the horizontal rectangle of an overdoor, within which is painted Ceres surrounded by agricultural implements (plate 36).

The decorative unity of the loggia extends above the walls to include the wooden structure of the ceiling (plate 18), which links the elements of the mural order with decorated architraves imitating marble, while the coffered compartments—sharply inset between progressively deeper cornices—pair off, almost in shadow, the sacrificial symbols of the bucrania and paterae (plates 37-38) and are closed by barely perceptible rows of ovolo and foliated acanthus ornaments.

In the vestibule a marble dado with classical motifs (plates 41-42, 44, 47-48)—which is repeated on the principal surfaces of the hall—picks up the theme of ceremonial enclosure already encountered on the sides of the loggia.

Together with the marbled enclosures on the long walls at the sides of the hall (plates 49, 51, 59), a columnar order reappears in the most elegant Corinthian form (plates 45, 49, 51, 59), equal in size to that of the loggia; two columns are in the center and two piers at the extremities, the latter integrated with the architectonic structure of the adjoining walls.

On the hall's southern or entrance wall, with the exception of the triumphal arch (plate 46) which the painter has elaborated as a magnificent frame for the access vault, the decoration shows but little change with respect to the rear wall of the loggia: to the sides of the arch one modification presents the cornices of the windows surmounted by curvilinear pediments (plates 46, 47, 48, 62, 63), above which a large shell forms the background for the bust of an emperor, placed on a projecting bracket in the middle of the architrave.

As in the atrium, scenes with trophies, statues, and giants are also painted in the intercolumniations above the marbled enclosure in the hall (plates 49, 51). Since this sequence, as it were, fills the proscenium, these compendious histories of "romana virtus" can be considered as a dramatic curtain which divides the great theatre-like space from the actual "scenes" in the adjacent rooms.

In the hall the connection between the columns is again accomplished, as in the loggia, by beams crossing in the ceiling (plates 45, 49, 51, 59) to form similar coffers, which appear even deeper with respect to the architecture because of the more evident projection of the crossing beams.

The northern rooms (plates 68-69, 73, 75, 78) have an analogous decorative arrangement, afforded by a screen of Ionic columns sustaining an entablature without a frieze. The trabeation articulates the room with four columns on each wall, enframing a door and a window in the central intercolumniation on the shorter sides, and on the long sides, a door and two arches in which are inserted scenes from the myths of Venus and Hercules. In the spandrels Zelotti placed imitation relief figures of winged Victories or of river gods (plates 68-69, 76-77).

The decoration of the southern rooms is disciplined by an architectonic structure which in certain ways repeats the images of the "pergulae" (plates 79, 81, 94, 96). Since these spaces are opened outward by three windows and two doors, the painter has created six more compartments illusionistically open, each corresponding in width to the three real windows. At the center of each wall, between the illusionistic apertures and also between the real ones, he composes a tall "tabernacle" motif with a pediment broken at the bottom to accommodate an arcuated cornice or a lunette (plates 79-81, 89, 94-96).

At the same time, these two rooms can certainly be compared to a sunny veranda in which one moves about, and by which one also enters the adjacent chambers of grotesques; there, apart from the decorative frames of the three doors, the only ornaments are foliated panels containing emblems and allusions, perfectly adapted to the smaller spaces. The flowering tendrils strung up with red ribbons, which form the borders of the symbolic gardens here depicted, are jasmine and rose, as in the admonitions of the rustic songs of the surrounding countryside which allude to the tragi-comic vicissitudes of fecundity and death (see Appendix II; plates 108-116, 118).

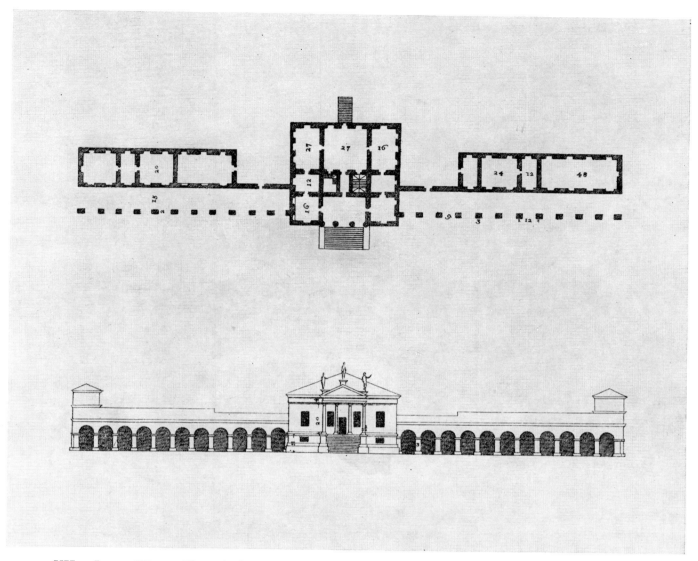

VII - ISAAC WARE, *Plan of the main floor and façade elevation of the Villa Emo at Fanzolo.*
From *The Four Books of Andrea Palladio's Architecture*, London, 1738, II, pl. XXXIII

THE LOGGIA

The two paintings at the sides of the loggia represent a symbolic contest which unites motifs of the love and downfall of Callisto with those of the cult of Diana and her "furious troop," [16] as well as the motifs of rural fertility in concord with the elements, together with the origins and ultimate historic mission of the house of Emo. The scenes representing the myth [17] divide the events into two periods: the first showing the amorous adventure of Callisto and Jupiter, disguised as Diana (plates 37, 39) but indicated by the emblem beside him of the eagle with the thunderbolts in his beak, the second showing the vengeance of Juno, accompanied by a peacock (plates 38, 40), who punishes the beautiful nymph, striking her with her fist and transforming her into a bear. But the attentive Jupiter protects his beloved maiden, assigning her a heavenly throne among the stars, so that the Thunderer, after having provoked with his passion the encounter of the primal elements of the earth—Fire and Air—grants a place to the fertility which triumphs in the figure of Ceres. The latter is placed over the architrave of the entrance portal (plates 35-36), as signifying the agricultural enterprise of Leonardo Emo. The Emo family, represented by Juno and the peacock (which appears as an Emo *impresa* in the loggia pavement), here advertised a warning that they had effectively assumed the goddess's office of retributive justice.[18]

The two scenes, which have no precedents in Zelotti's art, succeed brilliantly: the images, sharp and clear in their almost sculptural character, are illuminated fundamentally by the contrast of their colors, as they are immersed in an atmosphere rendered particularly vibrant by a sky irridescent with blue and rose. Ceres (plate 36) holds her sceptre amid the implements of agriculture—the rustic cart, rake, plow, hoe, and spade. Her hair is formed by ears of grain; her wine-red flesh tones contrast with the blue sky, varied by rosy clouds. The luminous power of this picture springs from the chromatic contrasts of the drapery—interwoven with orange-yellow, lilac, and white—and from the metallic reflections on the farm equipment, set off by the flesh tones of the figure and the variegated sky. The cascades of flowers, fruits, and foliage play off against the whiteness of the columns.

Above the cornices of the upper windows are set two female busts of tawny bronze (plate 35), backed by shells. One is Juno, recognizable by the arrangement of her hair with a diadem on top, as in the corresponding figure of the vengeance scene; the other is perhaps Jupiter in the semblance of Diana.

THE VESTIBULE

From the sides of the loggia the simulated marble dado (plates 37-38) runs into the vestibule (plates 41-42, 44, 47-48), where the ornamental Greek meander is transformed in the characteristic recessed frieze: thus the invitation to proceed receives encouragement from this detail, which presses at one's heels in the guise of marine waves.

Into the clear background of each side wall are inserted two doors, one real and the other painted. In the middle, niches framed by the standard tabernacle motif, with broken-bottomed pediments and laughing rams' head masks, contain imitation bronze statues of Conjugal Love—or an allegory of happy marriage, with two united hearts enflamed (plate 41)—and of Household Economy, with a roll of accounts (plate 42). The two statues are wrapped in Roman gowns and mantles. Conjugal Love has the typical facial type of Parmigianino, with a pointed chin and sketchy eyes and ears, and a satiric stamp no less suggestive than that of the figure opposite, whose aspect unexpectedly associates the features of an ephebe with a wavy spiral coiffure.

Above the dado is a pergola of vines (plate 43) supported by a wooden trellis. A winged putto—foreshortened against a blue sky, on rosy banks of clouds—scatters red and white flowers. The vines are loaded with clusters of grapes, and their leaves have taken on an autumnal coloring: sere and yellow, matured almost to overripeness, they join the entrance portal to the access arch of the great hall (plate 44).

The trellised arbor, though hardly refined in its details—perhaps the many restorations have destroyed its original parts—has a structure whose function is interesting as the scaffolding to a barrel vault (plates 44, 47-48). Meanwhile, on reaching the vestibule one encounters two complete figures of simulated bronze, whose decorative character brings them close to the numismatic quality of the busts in the loggia.

THE HALL

Passing through the access arch into the hall (plate 44), the motif most immediately apparent—especially for its contrast with the interlocking rhythms of the marble dado and Corinthian columns—is afforded by the powerful figures of prisoners (plates 49, 51, 53-58), who overhang the ledge of the cornice on which they lie.

In the middle intercolumniations, two history paintings[19] allude to the core of the drama presented in the villa, that is, to the " virtus romana," which recurs as perpetual admonition to the man bound up with his own affairs. One panel represents the magnanimity of Scipio (plates 49-50), who restores a maiden to her fiancé, Luteius (commonly called Aluccio), and to her father, to whom he also returns the price of her ransom counted out in pieces of gold.[20] The other scene represents the resolute will of the father of Virginia, who kills his own daughter (plates 51-52) rather than allowing her, as victim of the rapacious decemvir Appius Claudius, to surrender her maidenly virginity.[21]

The historic theme is by no means new to sixteenth-century villa decorations; Zelotti himself had already treated it elsewhere, while he had also turned the specific subject of the continence of Scipio, one belonging to a common iconographic repertory, to his own use in the Castle Da Porto-Colleoni at Thiene. Almost contemporaneously it had been used at Brugine, in the Villa Roberti, and later in the southern room of the villa at Caldogno.[22] But there is an evident diversity in the Villa Emo between these historical themes and those from mythological subjects presented in the other rooms. The mythologies, in fact, are manneristically developed in an almost archaizing atmosphere which presages the sorrowful, romantic yearning of a recherche du temps perdu. The historical theme reveals instead a stylistic adherence to the classical tradition of the Venetian schools, which in Zelotti's rendering seems typically more concrete and immediate.

In the four niches at the sides of the two stage scenes, with their piled-up trophies and prisoners crowning the marble dado, stand statues of imitation bronze representing the gods: Jupiter with his thunderbolts (plate 53), Juno with her peacock (plate 54), Neptune with a dolphin (plate 55), and Cybele with a lioness (plate 56)—also alluding to the primal elements of Fire and Air, Water and Earth. Above the statues, almost as if engraved, are gemlike allegories of the cardinal virtues as moral symbols, sublimating the terrestrial vicissitudes unfolded in the individual orchestration of the lavish corner decorations: from human bondage—the subjugated prisoners (plates 53-56) flanked by trophies —the free elements of nature encourage an emulation of the heights of virtue, as a gradual reassumption of rationality and even of divinity.

An examination of these details provides a better definition of the painter's style, which by the middle of the century had confidently incorporated numismatics, medals, seals, and reliefs. By his delight in amassing precious things within these compositions flanking the scenes of Roman virtue, and by his lively interest in sculptural modeling as displayed in the figures of the prisoners, with their Michelangelesque borrowings (plates 53-58), one recognizes with what sympathy Zelotti participated in the problematic formulations of Mannerism.

The corner decorations of the hall, beneath the trophies, elements, and virtues, are completed by a series of triumph friezes the color of tawny bronze (plates 64-67) set within the marble dado, to which they give light and by which they, too, are illuminated.[23]

Military trophies (plates 53-56) are piled against the Corinthian columns beside the Michelangelesque nudes on the cornice of this marble enclosure, the richness of their details offering a touch of fantasy as a framing element for the brazen figures of the four pagan divinities of the earth. They are composed of arms, banners, and shields with allusions to victories over the Turks, French, and Germans, referring to Leonardo Emo's exploits on land and sea. Flanking these decorations, other modelings and carvings are inserted orthogonally in groups at the extremities of the remaining shorter sides of the hall, in which the windows are also located. In place of the small windows aligned on axis above the larger ones, over the corresponding large blind windows in the hall there are instead two casements enframing painted panels (plates 59, 62-63), simulating light blue chalcedony with carved white figures from the myths of Apollo and Daphne (plate 62)[24] and the challenge of Marsyas to Apollo (plate 63)[25]—gemlike little scenes of marvelous quality.

Below the myth of Apollo pursuing Daphne is represented a bronze bust of the philosopher-emperor Marcus Aurelius, bearded and with curly hair, wearing a cuirass and mantle; below that of the contest between Apollo and the satyr Marsyas, held in the presence of the elderly Midas, whose royal features are shown changing into those of an ass, appears the bald, beardless, aristocratic, and uncompromising portrait of Julius Caesar, also armed and mantled (plates 46, 59, 62-63).

In corresponding positions on the opposite wall are depicted two other imperial busts, which are not easy to identify; above them are the two small open windows (plate 45). While one of the emperors appears in a Praxitelean mode, adolescent and beardless, the other, also beardless, is of more mature age. These char-

acteristics of the four imperial busts may also allude to the cycle of the ages of man and thus may stand as an analogy to the meaning of the primal elements—the statues of the four divinities—which they follow and with which, together with the Michelangelesque prisoners as equally allusive personifications of the four continents, they are integrated.

The hall's height seems extended by the triumphal arch (plate 46), which is the festive frame of the vestibule's arcuated vault; on its pediment (color plate *b*) recline the full-bodied figures of Prudence (plate 60), who holds a mirror in which her profile is reflected, and Abundance (plate 61) with a full cornucopia: *décolletées* in their dress, rainbow-hued and dissonant.

On the crown of the pediment—exactly opposite the Vittorian arms of the Emo family—is a mocking, vine-wreathed, comic mask (plate 46; color plate *b*) in simulated stone. Reflecting it, imitation sculptures above the mythological panels (and their corresponding windows) depict the bearded faces of satyrs and rams' heads seen in profile (plates 46, 60-63), bound by purple-blue fillets from which descend festoons of wild roses—whose cascade continues from the intercolumnar pediment brackets, multicolored and rich against the chalcedonies and the gilded statues of the gods.

THE STANZA DI ERCOLE

The scenes presented here relate to the loves of Hercules, who after having given valiant proof of his fortitude and rationality, became so muddled by love as to lose his wits. The other, parallel drama—in the corresponding room on the east—unfolds the story of Venus hopelessly enamored of the youthful Adonis.

Boccaccio's *De Genealogia* recounts the

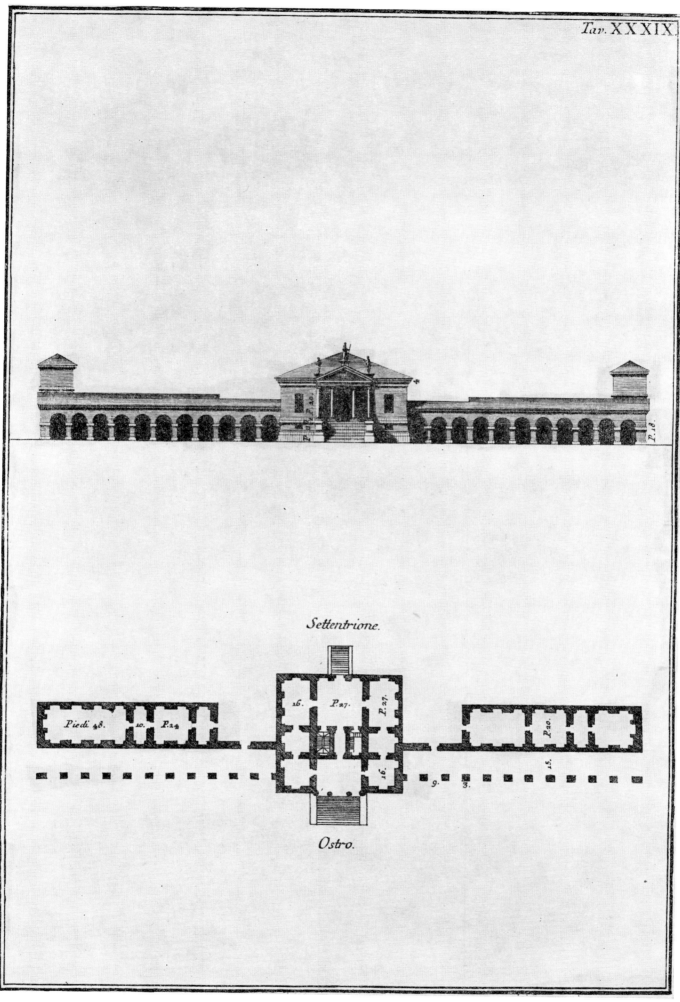

Settentrione.

Ostro.

VIII - FRANCESCO MUTTONI, *Façade elevation and plan of the main floor of the Villa Emo at Fanzolo.*
From *Architettura di Andrea Palladio Vicentino*, Venice, 1744, V, pl. XXXIX

vicissitudes of the hero's love [26] for Deianeira (plate 69-70), of his killing of the
centaur Nessus, and of his final madness
in which, uncontrollable, he first punishes
Lichas by hurling him into the sea (plate
71) and then orders his own cremation
atop a funeral pyre (plate 68): these form
the successive subjects of Zelotti's presentation. But the cycle also recalls Hercules'
labor in the husbanding of water and its
systematization for the benefit of lands and
crops. [27] A clear allusion is thus made to
the work of the Emo family for the irrigation of their lands, in the process of
building their residence at Fanzolo: further
allegories also allude to this enterprise, in
the recurrent images of river gods painted
in the spandrels above the three mythological scenes.

Over the door leading to the hall is
depicted the figure of Fame (plate 72;
color plate *d*) informing the world of the
events of the drama, having collected at
her own feet the lion-skin and quiver of
the deified hero. In the other overdoor
there is a Christian image (plate 73) within
a rich Sansovinesque frame of yellow-gold,
showing a rustic enclosure with the penitent Magdalene visited by Christ in the
aspect of a gardner, for whom her love,
once terrestial and fugitive, is transmuted
and made eternal. In the open intercolumniations, suspended by violet ribbons, hang
cascades of flowers, foliage, and fruits,
among which project russet apples, field
daisies, pomegranates, citrons, plums, and
ears of corn, within myriad sprays of red
and white wild roses.

The two largest Hercules panels, which
Zelotti had painted with almost identical
compositions at Brugine and at the Malcontenta, [28] here have an impressive breadth
in their tranquil landscape backgrounds.
They lack vigorous or incisive accents, in
that the figures are not generally involved
in dynamic action. A faded tonality char-

acterizes the religious panel; the elegance
of its images and the delicacy of its landscape do not offset a certain static vacuity.
The shortened concluding scene over the
fireplace—in which Hercules burns on the
pyre prepared by Philoctetes—achieves a
heightened power, because of the Mannerist pose of the hero and the tumult of
the infinite tongues of flame rising through
the various levels of the pyre.

Crystalline in her chiseled profile is the
magnificent figure of Fame (plate 72; color
plate *d*), who rests obliquely against the
variegated marble wall: the extraordinarily
elegant, luminous figure leans out in a
subtle undulation against the concavity of
her wings and is articulated in a move-
ment whose complexity is developed with
spontaneous ease. From the Fame, one's
eye passes easily to the little images of
the rivers in the spandrels of the Hercules
pictures, pouring out water from full leather
skins; they are reminiscent of the images
which Giovanni Maria Falconetto, also a
sculptor and medalist, placed as delicate
ornaments on his buildings, [29] and we find
them again, with the same vivid handling,
in the varied motifs of the Victories in
the Stanza di Venere. [30]

THE STANZA DI VENERE

On spacious backgrounds suffused with
violet and rose unfolds the other drama
of Venus and Adonis (plate 75). The familiar classical and Boccaccian tales provided the inspiration for the scenes; [31] but
the theme of love, conceived in fertile
hope, exhausts itself with eroticism in an
elegiac conclusion.

The scenes, analogous to those of Hercules, are three: the departure of Adonis
for the hunt, detained by Venus' attempt
to seduce him (plate 77); the discovery
of the dead Adonis (plate 76), found by

e - G. B. Zelotti: *Allegory of Architecture* (northern wall in the Stanza delle Arti)

the panic-stricken goddess through the baying of the hounds; and, above the fireplace, Venus pierced by the arrow of Love (plate 74), which might constitute either the inception or the conclusion of the trilogy. The pagan images of Love finally exhausted by its own excess combine allusions to the cycle of the seasons and thus repeat the sacred theme of permanence and transcendence.

In the tightly organized scene of Venus pierced by the arrow of Love, we find repeated the diagonal of the Fame from the cycle of Hercules. The goddess's unusual color is due not only to a different attitude on Zelotti's part, but also to the action of time in eroding the pigments, thus altering into pastel a composition that has largely been deprived of its original characteristics.

Zelotti reproduces on the opposite wall a gilded bust of Venus (plate 75), at the center of a rich and complicated decoration above the door giving onto the central hall. The bust rests on a bracket and is silhouetted against a concave shield, crowned by two dewy-eyed putti with garlands of fruits and flowers. As a redemption to the drama of Venus, there appears in the remaining overdoor, within a Sansovinesque frame, the sacred scene of the penitent St. Jerome in the desert (plate 78), which suggests an asceticism opposed to the vicissitudes of Love. In this picture—as well as in that of the Magdalene in the Stanza di Ercole—the bare, limitless extent of the landscape is especially admirable, imparting a breadth unusual in Zelotti's compositions.

In the spandrels of the arches are winged-Victory reliefs reminiscent of Falconetto (plates 76-77), and on the keystones of the arches are satyr masks wrapped in diviners' hoods. In the narrow intercolumniations of the short walls descend the usual cascades of fruits, foliage, and flowers

(plate 78), ever more abundant, in which we may note pine cones, figs, cherries, citrons, lemons, artichokes, and gourds. In the garland to the right of the door leading into the chamber of grotesques, we find again the motif of ears of corn among festoons of garden produce such as onions, garlic, and cucumbers.[32]

THE LYCEUM, OR STANZA DELLE ARTI

The Stanza delle Arti is the particularly personal room of the owner, since—apart from the presence of his portrait (plate 89) in the "divining lunette"[33] opposite a picture of the Holy Family (plate 88) transcending the human virtues—we find here the images of the humanistic Arts (plates 79, 82-87) in which Leonardo Emo and his age believed, even when the era of a new reality was already near. Models by Veronese provided the evident inspiration for the Holy Family, a religious subject which occurs also at Maser; but the quality of Zelotti's work is obviously much lower.

In this room, Zelotti produced in effect a succession of pictures. The familiar types prevail, with their affected poses, the sunless rosy-blue skies, the juxtapositions of wine-red with blue and orange with yellow, and the imposing female figures with flesh tones of violet and rose. The same may be said for the high frieze which runs beneath the beams. It is a sequence of festoons rich with wild flowers and foliage and tied with violet ribbons (plates 90-93), sometimes supported by winged putti, or conversely providing a perch for them, which they sit upon or straddle.

Over the fireplace between the two windows on the western wall and in the overdoor toward the loggia, two allegories of Winter (plate 81) and Summer (plate 80) are placed within niches. Painted in yellow ochre, so as to differentiate them from the other figures, they succeed handsomely through their sculptural quality and medallic sharpness. The figure of Winter is particularly fine, wrapped in a cloak which completely envelops him and partially hides his face. Equally felicitous is the figure of Summer, seated with her bust exposed, appearing to project slightly from her niche. She also wears shiny ears of grain in her hair, and a sheaf of wheat stands by her side. These images of the seasons recall in their *ensemble* an analogous, though lost, Zelottian scheme of 1557,[34] formerly in the Palazzo Trevisan at Murano.

The Stanza di Giove e di Io

Here the myth of Jupiter's vain love for Io is represented, as discovered and punished by Juno (plates 94, 98-103), thus recalling the other vengeance of Juno (represented in the loggia), where the goddess pummels and transforms the nymph Callisto, whom Jupiter had also seduced and made pregnant. The myth is adopted directly from Betussi's popular translation of the *De genealogia deorum* of Boccaccio.[35]

The pagan allegory finds its sublimated justification in the Christian image of the *Ecce Homo* (plates 94, 97), guiding mankind toward salvation through an acceptance of the tragic condition of life. The sacred scene, placed in an overdoor like a canvas in oils within a gilded frame, suggests precisely this iconographic connection, with the tragic mythologies around it, although it is stylistically different from the Olympian myths. But the pagan allegory also contains within itself an allusion to Jupiter's (the sun's) love of Io, that is, "l'humidità naturale del senso umano," begetting man and establishing him on earth. With this latent meaning the pagan symbol, grafted onto the Christian one, concludes with a cyclical-seasonal vision of continued renewal.

The six scenes,[36] which unfold in a mythical atmosphere against ample, open backgrounds, are connected stylistically and by the depth of their landscapes with the two sacred overdoors of the penitent St. Jerome and the apparition of Christ to Mary Magdalene in the garden. Also interesting in this ambience is the inclusion of the seasons painted in yellow ochre, the Spring (plate 95) and Autumn (plate 96) equinoxes concluding the cycle of the solstice from the Stanza delle Arti. The motif of Autumn repeats to the letter Ridolfi's description of the monochrome in Palazzo Trevisan at Murano,[37] with a peasant boy squeezing bunches of grapes. Equally successful is the statue of Spring, on whose slightly foreshortened, Parmigianinesque head brilliant flowers are interlaced. The simplicity of the lower part of the figure recalls antique sculptural solutions, while her bodice and lap are emphasized by rippling folds of drapery and the nervous flutter of her gown.

In the other frieze beneath the beams, within warmly gilded Mannerist frames, appear a series of gems of bluish jasper showing female dancers (plates 104-107) flung down in lascivious poses—now turning their backs, now facing outward, here swathed in a provocative reserve, there sprawling and foolish under the open pavilions of their cubicles, which exhale wisps of incense as an erotic invitation. They are the gems of illicit loves, those of antique— or, better, Alexandrine—carvings in which the hetairae display their allurements in sequence, here restated by the deft and easy hand of Zelotti.

The chambers of grotesques

At Fanzolo the grotesques, at once symbolic and emblematic, are arranged in floreated panels (plates 108-116; color plate *f*).[38] Each chamber has two identical configurations on the north and south walls, which relate to each other by means of a diagonal disposition within the diminutive architectural box. Thus the eastern chamber depicts on its north wall the symbols of earth, or Persephone, and of water, or Amphitrite, which are repeated obliquely on the opposite wall. The western chamber displays instead the symbols of fire, or Divination, and of air, or Priapus.

The ideal conjunction of the chambers is expressed by means of two common symbols: that of the Balance, painted on the walls leading to the stairs and vestibule, and that of Time and Poetry on the outer walls on the east and west, where the original windows, now transformed into doors leading to the wings, were located.

The Balance

Beside the head of a bearded soothsayer with a headdress of veils and plumes (plates 110, 115), upon long flowered stems of fennel and red ribbons, fertility motifs are symmetrically disposed, including satyrs (plate 119), bronzed herms with baskets filled with fruits and flowers on their heads, and the flaming torch and quiver, symbols of love. In the center is a large plaque with a soothsayer, enframed by two Harpies whose long necks are intertwined, (an heraldic image of shrew-like, miserly economy); on the plaque is depicted in red carnelian an evanescent spirit " in camisa," who performs the rite of augury with a flaming brazier (plate 115).

Beneath this symbol is a support composed of the long, thin arms of a balance whose fulcrum is a female herm wrapped in a veil, impassive of aspect, nude to the waist and cuirassed below. At the ends of the balance hang two weights stamped with images: one depicting the future reign of peaceful arts, the other the

ascendancy of violence and death. Two heraldic panthers, symbols of potential fertility, are overhung by festoons loaded with fruit, while two flittering dragonflies suggest the rapidity of change and the facile variation of the weights.

All these allegories are spread across a white field, against which their refined and delicate details take on brilliance and relief. When cameos or jaspers are incorporated into these settings the engraved figures assume enchanting aspects, combining with their precision the fantasy of a metaphysical investigation.

Fire, or Prophetic and Propitiatory Divination

At the sides of a tiny temple, two supplicant soothsayers (plates 108, 111) interrogate a spirit of the deceased, invoked in the flames of an altar. The soul appears as a brazen statue on the pediment of the temple, with its head silhouetted against a white circle enframed by a wide webbing stretched between staves; from these descend festoons of fruit, which in this case are tied to stalks of the unfortunate millet or " red sorghum," which two hungry birds approach to steal the seeds. The divination is rendered evident everywhere, even in the delicate support, by unguent amphorae and lamps (instruments used to foster the rites), while incense circulates to counteract the exhalations of Harpies, who attempt to confound the responses. At the bottom, exactly on axis with the symbolic elements already described, hangs a gem upon which is engraved a lightning bolt.

Water, or Amphitrite

From two satiric masks a prophetic baldachin is suspended; at its extremities two putti with dragonflies' wings hold lines on which hang three fish, strung up on their hooks, and two tortoises, "inhabitants of

Tartarus" (color plate *f*). Beneath the pavilion is represented the triumph of Amphitrite, with the goddess guiding a dolphin by its tail; the oceans and rivers (that is, the obelisks surmounted by globes with three flames) flank her apotheosis, while a pergola with red and green branches of pomegranate enframes her figure. At the sides, the usual magic unguent-jars exude their perfumes.

Underneath, on a gem within a richly wrought setting, is the image of a figure which tempts the water from a stream, leaning on a staff with her gown held up; this is a spirit of Prudence (plate 120). From this noble stone hangs the horrible head of Medusa (plate 121), enchantress of the snaky locks, at large upon the seas. But on the sides of this malignant image stand two trophies of war—emblems of victory at sea—in which are intermingled shields, mantles, admirals' staffs, lances, and plumed helmets. The symbolism may also be understood as an emblematic allusion to the governorship of the Emo over the oceans and rivers.

Earth, or Persephone

Beside a prophetic mask which emerges from the subterranean realms (plates 116, 118), indicated by snails and centipedes, appear the auspicious images of winged Amorini suspending bunches of fruits and flowers. At the center of the symbol is the triumph of Persephone, or Earth, under a pergola of pomegranates (plate 117). She leans on a thyrsus wreathed with fruits and foliage, holds a plate full of fruits, and is adorned with a garland of flowers. From her pavilion paterae and amphorae hang as trophies, alternating with flowery bouquets. Among painted butterflies two twining satyrs are gymnastically disposed upon a sacred veil descending from the pedestal of the goddess, while the veil supports the useful stems of fennel—from

whose flowers, however, spring stalks of the unhappy sorghum. Below, at the center of the satiric dance (as a conclusion to the propitiatory symbol rendered evident by the lamps burning at the sides of the goddess's pavilion), hangs in an elegant heraldic cartouche a shield-shaped black stone on which is engraved, in a brilliant design, the white image of Death reaping his harvest with a scythe.

Air, or Pan

From a soothsayer's mask, covered with sacred veils from whose fringes hang human enchantments, two other fringed swathes spread outward to connect two cornucopias (plates 109, 112). Two female figures uphold branches of holly and festoons of fruits and flowers. Between them a great inset cameo depicts the usual interrogation of souls above the brazier; one appears already propitious for the revelation. Beneath stands a herm of Pan, patron of harmony, accompanied by satyrs who support his outstretched arms, flanked by their symbols of flute and pipes.

The figures of the two female dancers are typically Zelottian, in their opposing postures as well as in the ornamental detail of their dress, and especially in their animal-head buckles, which can be found as recurring motifs among the female figures at Villa Emo.

Time

This painted panel is oblong, since together with the original window it is connected with the image representing Poetry on the same wall, perhaps in a single symbol. In both of the chambers the painting is spoiled by the transformation of the earlier window into a door, communicating with the adjacent *barchesse*.

From the hoary skull of a goat, to whose horns is tied a red ribbon, descend two bound and crossed gray wings, the sleep-

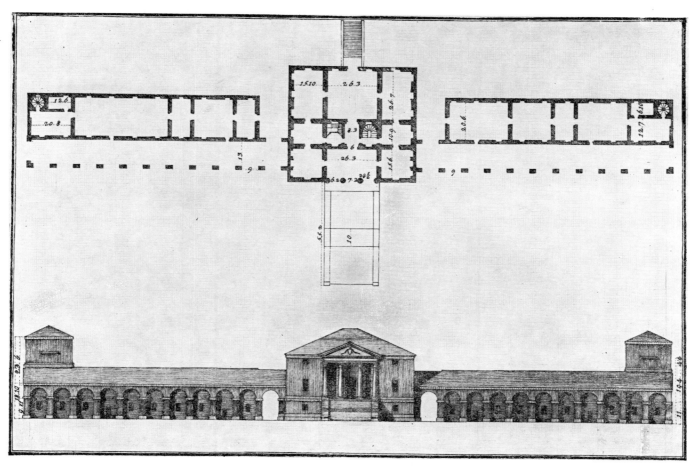

IX - ALESSANDRO MUCCI, *Plan of the main floor and façade elevation of the Villa Emo at Fanzolo.*
From *I Quattro Libri dell'Architettura di Andrea Palladio*, Siena, 1791, II, p. 105

ing head of a bearded prophet, two mallets, a clock with weights and bells, a terrestial globe, and an astrological manual. The elements of time thus recall each other through interconnection, by which the observer assimilates the concepts of scholastic, Aristotelian rhythm and astral flux as reinforced by the empirical Gregorian calculation, contradicted in its turn by the humanistic alternative whereby Time bears Truth in its flight or in its sleep: *Veritas filia Tempus est.*

Poetry

The symbol linked with that of Time, across the space of a window on the same wall, recalls the motif of the violet chalcedony in the hall with its contest of

Apollo and Marsyas (plate 113). Whereas there the Ovidian-Petrarchan image had symbolized prudence, by which the bestial should not contend with reason, here instead the emblems of lyric or Apollonian poetry—the lyre interlaced with laurel beneath the blond and radiant head of the god—are connected by the usual red ribbons descending from the head of a bearded and horned Silenus to emblems of rustic songs, symbolized by Marsyas flayed and transfixed, with his flute and bagpipe, upon branches of wild rose. A mediation between the two past rivals, now pacified, is evident in the purple prophetic veil which links the modest to the sublime, the coarse expression of the peasant to the speech and song of the noble.

NOTES

[1] Palladio, 1570, II, p. 55: " È stata ornata di pitture da M. Battista Venetiano "; Federici, 1803, II, p. 102: " ... Giambattista Zampezzi nato in Cittadella copiò con tutta esattezza i lavori ... del Zelotti in Fanzolo ... . "

[2] It was on the basis of a statement by Ridolfi (1648) that some scholars fell into the error of thinking that Paolo Veronese was also active at Fanzolo with Zelotti: among others, Dal Pozzo, 1718, p. 79; Crico, 1833, p. 124; Caliari, 1888, pp. 19, 294, 350; Foratti, 1914, p. 63; and Loukomski, 1927, p. 144.

[3] Von Hadeln, 1914, I, p. 364, n. 5; idem, 1914 (b), pp. 168 ff.; Fiocco, 1928, pp. 36-40, 205; Crosato, 1962, pp. 31 ff., 133 ff.; Pallucchini, 1968, pp. 203 ff. Further, on Zelotti in general: Venturi, in L'Arte, XXXII, 1929, pp. 49-67; E. Arslan, " Nota su Veronese e Zelotti," in Belle Arti, August-September 1948, pp. 227 ff.

[4] Cicogna, who possessed the fragments of the manuscript, discusses them in volume IV of the Iscrizioni veneziane, 1834, p. 409, mentioning an autograph marginal note by Palladio relating to the Villa Pisani at Montagnana, but not the other, relating to the Villa Emo: from the wording of this note he deduced that it had been made after 1567, and therefore dated the frescoes from 1567 to 1570. Von Hadeln, 1914, in his note on Ridolfi, agreed with some reserve to the chronology discovered by Cicogna, observing that Palladio's silence need not be held to account since, for example, he does not mention Paolo's frescoes at Maser. Zorzi, 1955, pp. 96 ff., in treating the manuscript fragments of I Quattro Libri dell'Architettura preserved in the Biblioteca del Museo Correr at Venice, established their dating between 1561 and 1565, with that of the autograph note after 1565 and before 1570—affirming that the decoration of the Villa Emo could only have taken place during these years.

[5] Pallucchini, 1968, p. 214.

[6] Fiocco, 1928 (rpt. 1934), pp. 26 ff.; R. Pallucchini, Mostra di Paolo Veronese (Catalogue), Venice, 1939, pp. 36-43; G. Bordignon Favero, La Soranza di Michele Sanmicheli e gli affreschi di Paolo Veronese, 1955, pp. 40-44 and plate VI.

[7] Pallucchini, 1968, p. 206.

[8] G. Vasari, Le vite dei più eccellenti pittori ..., Florence, 1568; ed. Ragghianti, 1943, III, p. 123. Ridolfi, 1648; ed. Von Hadeln, 1914, I, p. 299. Cf. F. Barbieri, " Gli affreschi cinquecenteschi del Castello Colleoni at Thiene," in Questa è Vicenza, 1952.

[9] Crosato, 1962, p. 123, proposed a dating toward 1557 for the frescoes of Villa Godi.

[10] F. Barbieri, Il Museo Civico di Vicenza, Venice, 1962, I, pp. 50-51.
Sources: Ovid, The Metamorphoses (II, 401-495); cf. Les Métamorphoses, Paris, 1961, pp. 50-54. G. Boccaccio, La genealogia degli Dei gentili con la spostazione de' sensi allegorici delle favole, et con la dichiarazione dell'historie appartenenti a detta materia. Tradotta per me Giuseppe Betussi da Bassano, 1559 (V, p. 99 r).

[11] B. Fiandrini, Memorie storico-cronologiche dell'insigne Monastero di S. Maria di Praglia (manuscript in the Museo Civico at Padua, BP-127-VI), 1800, p. 39 b; Dal Bosco, 1959-60, pp. 63 ff.

[12] As Pallucchini has observed (1968, p. 214), the mythological episode of Juno striking Callisto has "stylistic affinities with one of the panels of the library ceiling, the Bishop Scourging Heretics, or with the canvas of 1562 in the Duomo of Vicenza showing the Conversion of St. Paul."

[13] Sources: Petrarch, De viris illustribus (Life of Scipio, 5-7; Florence, 1964, I, pp. 163-164, 330. The episode recurs in the Lettere senili (II, 1). Cf. Petrarch, Prose, Milan and Naples, 1965, p. 1060. Petrarch read the episode in Livy (XXVI, 50); Leipzig, 1909, pp. 172-173. Valerius Maximus, Factorum et Dictorum Memorabilium (IV, 3, 1); Leipzig, 1888, pp. 177-178. Frontinus, Strategemata (II, 11, 5); Leipzig, 1888, pp. 83-84.

[14] Sources: Petrarch, Triumphus pudicitiae (136-139); cf. Rime, trionfi e poesie latine, Milan and Naples, 1951, p. 514. G. Boccaccio, De mulieribus claris (LXXIV); ed. V. Zaccaria, Milan and Verona, 1967, p. 298. Livy (III, 48); Leipzig, 1908, I, pp. 187-188.
Wolters, in " Andrea Palladio e la decorazione dei suoi edifici", Bollettino del C.I.S.A., Vicenza, 1968, X, p. 255 ff., has observed how rarely Palladio arranged himself for the decoration of his villas.

[15] L. Magagnato, Teatri italiani del Cinquecento, Venice, 1954, p. 52.

[16] See page 53.

[17] Boccaccio, La genealogia ..., cit. See pp. 40, 53.
Sources: Ovid, Metamorphoses (I, 452-567, etc.); cf. Les Métamorphoses, cit., I, pp. 23-27. Petrarch, Rime (XXXIII, XXXIV); cf. Rime e trionfi, Milan, 1957, pp. 93, 551; idem, Triumphus cupidinis (154-156).

[18] The peacock is the emblem of the Emo family.
Source: Ovid, Metamorphoses (VI, 382-400); cfr. Les Métamorphoses, Paris, 1955, II, p. 15.

[19] See below.
Sources: Petrarch, Triumphus Amoris (I, 125); cf. Rime e trionfi, cit., p. 549. Boccaccio, La genealogia ..., cit., pp. 151, 155 r, 156. Sophocles, The Trachiniae; cf. Sophoclis fabulae (777 ff., 1254 ff.); Oxford, 1924. The Hercules incidents derive directly from Petrarch and Boccaccio, although they were reworked in 1557 at Modena in a poem by G. Giraldi Cinzio entitled L'Ercole. Seneca, Hercules Furens (635-639); Tragoediae, Leipzig, 1921, p. 20. Hercules Oeteus (1484-1517); ibid., pp. 375-376.

[20] Petrarch, Life of Scipio, cit. (5-7). The episode recurs in the Lettere senili (II, 1). Petrarch read the episode in Livy (XXVI, 50, 52); Valerius Maximus (IV, 3, 1); and Frontinus (II, 11, 5). The episode is described by Petrarch, and was later taken up again by Boccaccio.
Source: Boccaccio, La genealogia ..., cit., p. 151.

[21] Petrarch, Triumphus pudicitiae, cit., pp. 136-139. Boccaccio, De mulieribus claris, cit. (58).
Source: Livy (III); pp. 41 ff. The episode is similarly drawn from Petrarch and Boccaccio.

[22] Crosato, 1962, p. 195.

[23] See p. 40.

[24] Petrarch, Rime ..., cit.; Triumphus cupidinis, cit., pp. 154-156.
Sources: Ovid, Les Métamorphoses, Paris, 1961; Boccaccio, La genealogia ..., cit., II, p. 37 r.

[25] Boccaccio, La genealogia ..., cit.
Source: Ovid, Les Métamorphoses, cit.

[26] Petrarch, Triumphus cupidinis, cit., pp. 124-125. Boccaccio, La genealogia ..., cit., pp. 151, 155 r, 156.
Sources: Sophocles, The Trachiniae, cit.; see also note 19.

[27] Boccaccio, La genealogia ..., cit., p. 151.

[28] Crosato, 1962, pp. 92 ff.; pp. 136 ff.

29 CHECCHI-GAUDENZIO-GROSSATO, *Padova: Guida ai monumenti e alle opere d'arte*, Venice, 1961, pp. 265-266.
Sources: BOCCACCIO, *La genealogia*..., cit., I, pp. 123, 143. OVID, *Metamorphoses* (I, 583-746); cf. *Les Métamorphoses*, cit., I, pp. 27-33. AESCHYLUS, *Prometheus Bound*; cf. *Aeschili Tragoedie*, Oxford, 1937, pp. 127-133.

30 See p. 45.

31 BOCCACCIO, *La genealogia*..., cit., II, p. 37 r.

32 See p. 14.

33 See p. 53.

34 RIDOLFI, 1648, p. 261; DAL BOSCO, 1959-60.

35 BOCCACCIO, *La genealogia*..., cit., pp. 123, 143-144.

Sources: OVID, *Les Métamorphoses*, cit. AESCHYLUS, *Prometheus Bound*, cit.

36 The subjects depicted in the colonnade compartments are the following:
—Jupiter and Io seated, observed by Juno.
—Jupiter, surprised by Juno, transforms Io into a heifer.
—Juno consigning her rival to Argus.
—Mercury charming Argus to sleep.
—Mercury decapitating Argus.
—Triumph of Juno, drawn in her chariot.

37 RIDOLFI, 1648, pp. 309, 352 [translator's note].

38 See pp. 13-14.

APPENDIX II

THE SECT OF THE BENANDANTI

It is by no means a novelty that the decorative programs of Venetan villas unite Christian with mythological themes, or that this has sometimes been thought to reflect a kind of contradiction which has engendered some perplexity. At the Villa Emo, as well, the apparent contradictions are numerous— in fact the dialectic is perhaps more accentuated here than elsewhere (we might point out in passing the theatrical production of the time, or, at any rate, the theatrical representations which would have a reflection also in painting, especially in scenographic and decorative types).

The center of the literary world that involved the mural decoration of villas was at Castelfranco, gathered at the " Paradiso " of Queen Caterina Cornaro. At her court, Pietro Bembo was cardinal, not only of the humanistic culture of the Veneto, but of a specialized and then innovatory question: the affirmation of popular Italian, in imitation of Petrarch, as against the learned use of Latin. With Petrarch, Boccaccio was also reinvoked for his erudite Latinizing productions, especially as his Latin works came to be translated by the Petrarchists to demonstrate how the new linguistic form could lend itself to whatever theme one might wish.

The choice of the mythical subjects in the Villa Emo takes account of related agrarian allegories alluding to fertility and to the primal elements, which when they are in harmony render the land productive and when they are discordant fail to ripen the crops in the fields. All this was of considerable interest to the owner of the villa, even though the moral and religious content of the images may have predominated. Leonardo Emo, in fact, considered it necessary that upon the decadent, aristocratic eroticism which Aretino could document in detail there should be wrought a cure that could derive only from the responsibilities of a rustic life, and from that heavenly mercy which falls with especial abundance upon men of good will.

Together with the panel pictures and sacred images, the myths of the Villa Emo represent themes with both moral and agrarian allusions, while in the decorations of many other villas the iconographic schemes are not found to be related. At the Villa Emo there also appear decorative peasant symbols which form the necessary and essential element of a villa. In this connection, a conjunction of philological characteristics provides useful circumstantiation of certain meanings in relation to the grotesques, and particularly to the decorations of the loggia (which in some respects is external to the house) and of an arch above the southern window in the Stanza delle Arti (plate 89). This is the symbolism of anxiety which torments the farmer on the fate of his plantings, his works, and his crops, with regard to seasonal vicissitudes and unforeseeable events that bring damage to both harvests and people. The outcome for good or bad is told by the usefulness— or the harm—of the products which the peasant derives from the land, in a perpetual struggle whose origins lie in the first agrarian settlements; it was from earliest times accompanied by the need for cult magic in such prime farmlands as the Veneto, Friuli, and Emilia, where an extensive, flat plain favors the cultivation of cereals. There, surviving in remote areas even today, cult magic is perpetuated with conviction through secret peasant initiations transmitted from generation to generation. This is a sort of rustic religion, in which there appears a fundamental dissension between the demonic principle of waste, damage, irresponsibility, and destruction, as against the opposite one of economy, order, foresight, and careful conservation. Christianity has attempted since its beginnings in these areas to absorb such agrarian magic into its own rational workings, but has never succeeded in uprooting it from the profound irrationalism of the rustic soul.

This ancient magic was locally rekindled precisely in the middle of the sixteenth century, at which point there are notices of inquisitions and sentences related to it, carried out in the surroundings of Fanzolo, Asolo, and Castelfranco by the tribunal of the Holy Office on the general charge of Protestantism. But here there were no Protestants; instead, there arose in the wake of the Reformation an Anabaptist sect of poor peasants who revolted against the centralized government and the individual capitalist. The outbreak of heresy spread through these wretched districts and took especial hold on the oppressed, rousing against such forces the laboring population, who scrutinized events and interrogated the future in order to husband carefully the wages, the

f - G. B. ZELOTTI: *Allegory of Water, or Amphitrite* (south wall in the eastern chamber of grotesques)

wine, and the bit of " red sorghum " which was conceded them.

Such was the heresy of the Benandanti, described with factual precision in a documentary study by C. Ginzburg,[1] which also mentions celebrated trials in the state of Friuli, where first Giovanni Emo and subsequently his son Leonardo had been governors for the Venetian Signoria. The heresy organized the resistance of the peasants against any sort of malign force (including that of the landowners, whenever they were not helpful or beneficent) by means of an elect group said to have been " nati con la camisa," that is, born under a particular planet. This group had the charge of combatting witches, sorcerers, and demons who gathered, around the time of the Ember days, in a designated place, for the purposes of destroying crops or to " magnare tutti li putti," concluding their furies with an orgy and cortège led by the goddess Diana. The latter, followed by her ministers, embarked upon a hunt, especially for wine in the cellars, to waste it or ruin it, wrenching open the " candole " of the casks—to the vexation of whoever might own or have charge of them—while " montando a cavalletto delle botti ... li strigoni ... bevuto che havevano, pisciavano dentro."

One notices also that the agrarian cult of the Benandanti must have been intimately connected with that of Diana and her " furious band." As we have seen, Diana is painted in the loggia of the Villa Emo as a form of exorcism, precisely because the reflection of her image and of her own feats would bind her as a spell against entering the cellars of the house to despoil its wines and grains.

When summoned to reunion by an irresistible superior force, the Benandanti (whose bodies became at the same time dissociated from their souls) were bound in thrall to an open struggle against orcs and witches. They could not join any witches' Sabbath nor any conclave of the Furies; they must never be turned by anyone from their charge; nor must their bodies be touched—or worse yet, turned over—during their actual " ecstasies." The evil spirits were armed with staffs of sorghum, while the " Benandanti " fought with long stems of flowering fennel. They possessed prophetic gifts through the interrogation of the deceased, arriving at a knowledge of the future fate of harvests and of men; hence the necessity of their communication with the dead, which took place on the feast day of the convocation of the departed. On the first of November the " Benandanti " were charged to join the dead souls in nocturnal processions within their cemetery walls. The deceased could also be invoked by the " benandante " spirit and interrogated, once it could be made to appear in the flame of a diviner's brazier.

The chambers of grotesques at the Villa Emo—which, among other things, I have considered as appropriate places for meetings between the owner and the overseer or peasants—each have a small fireplace within a stone frame. These cannot serve to heat the tiny rooms, especially since their openings (which are closed by wooden shutters against potential damage to the walls) are divided into three parts—the first for the flame, the second for the kindling, and the third for the pokers (plates 112, 118). These chambers might therefore be interpreted also as places of initiation into the interrogations of the dead, who would reappear in the flames of the miniature grates. The frescoed images, while alluding to divination or prophecy, express in every panel motifs of fecundity in contrast to malign elements, through which life is always a tragi-comic happening specifically comprehensible to the country-folk who are initiated into its mysteries. In the many cameos or in the gems which decorate the symbols of the grotesques appear the enchantress Gorgon with her snaky hair, Death with his scythe, the Prudence of a questing soul (trying with her toe the waters of a Stygian stream), a " Benandante " *nata con la camisa* (which billows up behind her, in the form of a halo) who interrogates one of the dead by the flame of a tiny altar. The weapons of the struggle—sorghum for the witches' brooms and the long stems of fennel—are depicted as well. Meanwhile, the symbolic image of each panel is dominated from above by the grinning face of a soothsayer or an eyeless mask, from whose veils, tied up in little sacks with crimson strings, hang the enchantments, the determining " planets," of human fate.

In conclusion to these observations, one cannot neglect the image of the lunette in the Stanza delle Arti, above its southern window (plate 89). It represents, within a ponderous setting, the foreshortened view of a spirit " in camisiola " as it is invoking the soul of one deceased, who appears in a dusky shade on the front of his own tomb. The invocation is requested (toward what response?) by a figure in the left foreground, perhaps kneeling, who implores the seers and the shades to prophesy and give him truth: it is a portrait of Leonardo Emo, already sorrowful and old, in the guise of an ancient warrior who will henceforth fight no more.

In the Stanza delle Arti this image is well placed, even by its reticence, in the midst of the figures of the Liberal Arts who here constitute a new theme, a profoundly significant humanistic presence. At the top, reigning alike over the human mind and all the Arts, is placed the Holy Family; before it, and on the same level, is set the supplicant image of the patron.

NOTE TO APPENDIX II

[1] C. Ginzburg, *I Benandanti—Ricerche sulla stregoneria e sui culti agrari tra Cinquecento e Seicento*, Turin, 1966.

BIBLIOGRAPHY*
for the architecture

MANUSCRIPT SOURCES

16th century " Libro rosso dell'Officio delle Acque di Treviso."
MS at the Consorzio Irriguo Brentella di Pederobba in
Montebelluna (Treviso), without collocation.

1561-65 A. PALLADIO, " I Quattro Libri di Architettura." MS
Cicogna 3617, Museo Correr, Venice.

1688 " Libro rosso dell'Officio delle Acque di Treviso." MS
(copy of the 16th-century original) at the Consorzio Irriguo
Brentella di Pederobba in Montebelluna (Treviso), without collocation.

1763 " Dissegno generale di tutta la Brentella ... ." Maps at the
Consorzio Irriguo Brentella di Pederobba in Montebelluna
(Treviso), without collocation, fols. 47-48.

PRINTED WORKS

1570 A. PALLADIO, I Quattro Libri dell'Architettura, Venice.

1726 G. LEONI, L'Architecture de Palladio, The Hague, vol. I,
bk. II, pl. XL.

1738 I. WARE, The Four Books of Andrea Palladio's Architecture, London, bk. II, pl. XXXIII.

1744 F. MUTTONI, Architettura di Andrea Palladio Vicentino,
Venice, vol. V, pl. XXXIX.

1776-83 O. BERTOTTI SCAMOZZI, Le Fabbriche e i Disegni di
Andrea Palladio raccolti e illustrati, Vicenza, vol. III.

1791 A. MUCCI, I Quattro Libri dell'Architettura di Andrea
Palladio, Siena, bk. II, p. 105.

1803 D. M. FEDERICI, Memorie trivigiane sulle opere di disegno, Venice, vol. II, pp. 72-73.

1822 L. CRICO, Viaggetto pittorico da Venezia a Possagno,
Venice, pp. 50-51.

1833 L. CRICO, Lettere sulle belle arti trivigiane, Treviso, pp.
138-140.

1844 C. FOPPIANI, Le fabbriche e i disegni di A. Palladio e
le terme, Turin, vol. III, pp. 33-36.

1847 Venezia e le sue lagune, Venice, I, 2ª, p. 171.

1855 J. BURCKHARDT, Der Cicerone, eine Anleitung zum Genus
der Kunstwerke Italiens, Basel (cf. 1952).

1864 G. B. SEMENZI, Treviso e la sua provincia, Treviso, pp. 166,
361-363.

1873 P. ANTONINI, Del Friuli e in particolare dei trattati da
cui ebbe origine la dualità politica in questa regione,
Venice.

1874 A. CACCIANIGA, Ricordo della provincia di Treviso, Treviso, p. 305.

1875 A. CACCIANIGA, " Villa Emo-Capodilista in Fanzolo," in
Illustrazione italiana, Milan, p. 154.

1880 V. BARICHELLA, Andrea Palladio e la sua scuola, Lonigo,
p. 34.

1890 D. BRENTARI, Da Treviso a Padova a Belluno e Feltre,
Bassano, p. 47.

1900 P. MOLMENTI, " La villa Emo a Fanzolo—la villa di un
patrizio veneto," in Emporium, January, pp. 25 ff.

1907 A. SERENA, Fra' Giocondo e il canale della Brentella,
Treviso.

1908 A. MARCHESAN, Notizie storiche ed artistiche su Fanzolo
e la sua chiesa, Treviso, pp. 38, 42.

1909 F. BÜRGER, Die Villen des Andrea Palladio, Leipzig, pp. 102-
104, pls. XXXIX-XL.

O. F. TENCAJOLI, " La villa Emo in Fanzolo," in Ars et
Labor, March, pp. 180-88.

1910 S. RUMOR, Breve storia degli Emo (first ed., Vicenza,
1887), Vicenza.

1911 M. R. HENARD, " La villa Emo," in Revue de l'art ancien
et moderne, pp. 193-206.

1913 S. ROMANIN, Storia documentata di Venezia, Venice (second
edition reprinted from original published in 1853-61),
vol. V, pp. 218, 295, 386-387.

1919 G. FAURE, La couronne de Venise, Paris, pp. 88-92.

1924 G. LUKOMSKIJ, Andrea Palladio, Munich (cf. 1927).

1926 G. K. LOUKOMSKI, Les villas des Doges de Venise, Paris,
pp. 4-5, 10.

1927 G. K. LOUKOMSKI, Les grands architects: Andrea Palladio,
Paris, pp. 89-90.

1928 P. MOLMENTI, La storia di Venezia nella vita privata, Ber-
gamo, vol. II, pp. 210-211.

1929 A. SERENA, Il canale della Brentella e le nuove opere di
presa e di derivazione nel quinto secolo dagli inizi, Treviso, pp. 28-29, 124-128.

1948 R. PANE, Andrea Palladio, Turin (cf. 1961).

1949 R. WITTKOWER, Architectural Principles in the Age of
Humanism, London (cf. 1962, 1964).

1952 G. MAZZOTTI, Le ville venete, Treviso (cf. 1954).

J. BURCKHARDT, Il Cicerone, guida al sentimento dell'arte
in Italia, Florence, p. 392 (cf. 1855).

1954 G. MAZZOTTI, Le ville venete, Treviso (3rd ed.), p. 717.

1956-57 G. FURLAN - I. MARTIN, " Villa Emo Capodilista a Fanzolo di Andrea Palladio," in Architettura, Milan, pp. 443-
447.

* Those studies which have direct and specific relevance to the architecture and pictorial decoration of Villa Emo
are listed in the general bibliographies. Others are given full citations in the notes and therefore are not entered
in the bibliographic lists.

1958   G. Mazzotti, *Le ville venete*, Rome, pp. 8, 106, 138.

1959   F. Franco, " Piccola e grande urbanistica palladiana," in *Bollettino del Centro Internazionale di Studi di Architettura "Andrea Palladio,"* I, p. 29.

1961   S. Branzi, " Splendore e miseria delle ville venete," in *Arte figurativa*, IX, no. 50, pp. 34-54.

      R. Pane, *Andrea Palladio*, Turin, pp. 223, 227, 229.

1962   G. Mazzotti, " Le ville venete e l'opera dell'Ente istituito per il loro restauro e conservazione," in *Giornale economico* della Camera di Commercio, Industria, e Agricoltura di Venezia, no. 7, pp. 819-820.

      R. Wittkower, *Architectural Principles in the Age of Humanism*, London (cf. 1949 and 1964).

1963   M. Salmi, " Rinascimento," *Enciclopedia universale dell'arte*, Venice-Rome, XI, s. v.

      B. Zevi, " Palladio," *Enciclopedia universale dell' arte*, Venice-Rome, X, pp. 447, 453-455

1964   R. Wittkower, *Principii architettonici nell'età dell'Umanesimo*, Turin, pp. 72-74, 76, 102-106, 124, 126-128.

1965   L. Balzaretti, *Ville venete*, Milan, p. 32.

      P. Bieganski, " I problemi della composizione spaziale delle ville palladiane," in *Bollettino del Centro Internazionale di Studi di Architettura "Andrea Palladio,"* VII, pt. 2, pp. 28-29.

1966   J. S. Ackerman, *Palladio*, Harmondsworth.

      M. Salmi, " Renaissance," in *Encyclopedia of World Art*, New York - London, XII, cols. 1-121.

      B. Zevi, " Palladio," in *Encyclopedia of World Art*, New York - London, XI, cols. 59-81.

1967   J. S. Ackerman, *Palladio's Villas*, Locust Valley (N. Y.).

      E. Forssman, " Tradizione e innovazione nelle opere e nel pensiero di Palladio," in *Bollettino del Centro Internazionale di Studi di Architettura "Andrea Palladio,"* IX, p. 253.

      N. Ivanoff, *Palladio*, Milan, pp. 46, 59, 62, 166.

      C. Semenzato, " Gli spazi esterni e il manierismo di Andrea Palladio," in *Bollettino del Centro Internazionale di Studi di Architettura "Andrea Palladio,"* IX, p. 344.

1968   P. Bieganski, " La struttura architettonica di alcune ville di Palladio in rapporto alla loro funzione pratica," in *Bollettino del Centro Internazionale di Studi di Architettura "Andrea Palladio,"* X.

BIBLIOGRAPHY
for the decoration

1570   A. Palladio, *I Quattro Libri dell'Architettura*, Venice.

1648   C. Ridolfi, *Le Meraviglie dell'Arte*, Venice, I, p. 350.

1718   B. Dal Pozzo, *Le vite dei pittori, degli scultori, degli architetti veronesi*, Verona, p. 79.

1803   D. M. Federici, *Memorie trivigiane sulle opere di disegno*, Venice, p. 110.

1822   L. Crico, *Viaggetto pittorico da Venezia a Possagno*, Venice, pp. 50-51.

1833   L. Crico, *Lettere sulle belle arti trivigiane*, Treviso.

1834   E. A. Cicogna, *Iscrizioni veneziane illustrate*, Venice.

1864   G. B. Semenzi, *Treviso e la sua provincia*, Treviso.

1874   A. Caccianiga, *Ricordo della provincia di Treviso*, Treviso, pp. 361-363.

1875   A. Caccianiga, " Villa Emo-Capodilista in Fanzolo," in *Illustrazione italiana*, Milan, p. 154.

1888   P. Caliari, *Paolo Veronese; sua vita e sue opere*, Rome.

1890   D. Brentari, *Da Treviso a Padova a Belluno e Feltre*, Bassano, pp. 47-48.

1900   P. Molmenti, " La villa Emo a Fanzolo—la villa di un patrizio veneto," in *Emporium*, January, pp. 24 ff.

1908   A. Marchesan, *Notizie storiche ed artistiche su Fanzolo e la sua chiesa*, Treviso.

1909   O. F. Tencajoli, " La villa Emo in Fanzolo," in *Ars et Labor*, March, pp. 180-188.

1910   S. Rumor, *Breve storia degli Emo* (1st ed., Vicenza, 1887), Vicenza, pp. 40-43 and pls. XX-XXIV.

1911   M. R. Henard, " La villa Emo," in *Revue de l'art ancien et moderne*, pp. 193, 206.

1914   D. von Hadeln, *Note al Ridolfi* (*Le Meraviglie dell'arte*, 1648), I, n. 5.

      A. Foratti, " Paolo Veronese nelle ville del Veneto," in *Rassegna d'arte*.

      D. von Hadeln, " Veronese und Zelotti," in *Jahrbuch der Königlich Preussischen Kunstsammlungen*, XV, pp. 168 ff.

1919   G. Faure, *La couronne de Venise*, Paris, pp. 88-92.

1926   G. K. Loukomski, *Les villas des Doges de Venise*, Paris, p. 10.

1927   G. K. Loukomski, " Les fresques de Paolo Véronèse et de ses disciples," in *Revue de l'art*.

1928   G. Fiocco, *Paolo Veronese*, Bologna.

      P. Molmenti, *La storia di Venezia nella vita privata*, Bergamo, II, pp. 210-211.

1929   A. Venturi, " Giambattista Zelotti," in *L'Arte*, XXXII.

      A. Venturi, *Storia dell'arte*, Milan, IX, 4ª, p. 976.

1936   B. Berenson, *Pitture italiane del Rinascimento*, Milan, pp. 521-547.

1947   L. Brenzoni, *Zelotti, Giovanni Battista*, in Thieme - Becker, *Allgemeines Lexicon der Bildenden Künstler*, Leipzig, XXXVI, p. 454.

1952   G. Mazzotti, *Le ville venete*, Treviso (cf. 1954).

1954   G. Mazzotti, *Le ville venete*, Treviso (3rd ed.), p. 717.

1955   G. G. Zorzi, " Contributo alla datazione di alcune opere palladiane," in *Arte Veneta*.

1958   G. Mazzotti, *Le ville venete*, Rome, pp. 138-139.

1959-60   M. Dal Bosco, *Giambattista Zelotti* (thesis, University of Padua, Istituto di Storia dell'Arte Moderna).

1962   L. Crosato, *Gli affreschi delle ville venete del Cinquecento*, Treviso, pp. 31 ff., 112 ff.

1963   F. Negri Arnoldi, " Prospettici e quadraturisti," in *Enciclopedia universale dell'arte*, Venice-Rome, XI, p. 105.

1965   L. Balzaretti, *Ville venete*, Milan, p. 32.

1966   F. de' Maffei, " Perspectivists," in *Encyclopedia of World Art*, New York - London, XI, cols. 221-243.

1967   J. S. Ackerman, *Palladio's Villas*, Locust Valley (N. Y.), p. 44.

1968   L. Magagnato, " I collaboratori veronesi di Andrea Palladio," in *Bollettino del Centro Internazionale di Studi di Architettura "Andrea Palladio,"* X, p. 170.

R. Pallucchini, " Giambattista Zelotti e Giovanni Antonio Fasolo," in *Bollettino del Centro Internazionale di Studi di Architettura "Andrea Palladio,"* X, pp. 203 ff.

B. Rupprecht, " L'iconologia nella villa veneta," in *Bollettino del Centro Internazionale di Studi di Architettura "Andrea Palladio,"* X, pp. 237-238.

INDEX OF NAMES AND PLACES

Proper names are in capitals; place names are in italics. Numbers refer to pages in the text. The abbreviation " n. " preceding a number within parentheses refers to the corresponding note on the page indicated.

FIGURES IN THE TEXT

PLATES

42   G. B. ZELOTTI: *Allegory of Household Economy* (vestibule)

43   G. B. ZELOTTI: *Grape-arbor with a Putto* (vestibule ceiling)

44   Villa Emo: access arch from the vestibule to the central hall

45   Villa Emo: northern end of the central hall, with the carved arms of the Emo family in the center

46   Villa Emo: entrance arch to the central hall, with decorations by G. B. Zelotti

47   Villa Emo: southern end of the central hall viewed from the left

48   Villa Emo: southern end of the central hall viewed from the right

49   G. B. ZELOTTI: frescoes on the western side of the central hall

50   G. B. ZELOTTI: *The Continence of Scipio* (middle zone, western side of the central hall)

51   G. B. ZELOTTI: frescoes on the eastern side of the central hall

52   G. B. ZELOTTI: *The Death of Virginia* (middle zone, eastern side of the central hall)

53   G. B. ZELOTTI: *Jupiter*, with a *Prisoner* beneath (left-hand zone, eastern side of the central hall)

54   G. B. ZELOTTI: *Juno*, with a *Prisoner* beneath (right-hand zone, eastern side of the central hall)

55   G. B. ZELOTTI: *Neptune*, with a *Prisoner* beneath (left-hand zone, western side of the central hall)

56   G. B. ZELOTTI: *Cybele*, with a *Prisoner* beneath (right-hand zone, western side of the central hall)

57   G. B. ZELOTTI: *Prisoner beneath Neptune's Niche* (left-hand zone, western side of the central hall)

58   G. B. ZELOTTI: *Prisoner beneath Cybele's Niche* (right-hand zone, western side of the central hall)

59   Villa Emo: overall view of the central hall; south wall on the right, east on the left

60   G. B. ZELOTTI: *Prudence* (over the entrance arch of the central hall)

61   G. B. ZELOTTI: *Abundance* (over the entrance arch of the central hall)

62   G. B. ZELOTTI: *Apollo and Daphne* (within panel); below, *Bust of Marcus Aurelius* (flanking the entrance arch of the central hall, on the left)

63   G. B. ZELOTTI: *The Contest of Apollo and Marsyas* (within panel); below, *Bust of Julius Caesar* (flanking the entrance arch of the central hall, on the right)

64-65   G. B. ZELOTTI: *Triumphs* (panels of the dado on the western side of the central hall)

66-67   G. B. ZELOTTI: *Triumphs* (panels of the dado on the eastern side of the central hall)

68   G. B. ZELOTTI: *Hercules on the Pyre* (western wall in the Stanza d'Ercole)

69   G. B. ZELOTTI: frescoes on the eastern wall in the Stanza d'Ercole

70   G. B. ZELOTTI: *Hercules and Deianeira before the Body of Nessus* (left-hand zone of the eastern wall in the Stanza d'Ercole)

71   G. B. ZELOTTI: *Hercules Preparing to Throw Lichas into the Sea* (right-hand zone of the eastern wall in the Stanza d'Ercole)

72   G. B. ZELOTTI: *Fame* (overdoor on the eastern wall in the Stanza d'Ercole)

73   G. B. ZELOTTI: *Noli me tangere* (overdoor on the southern wall in the Stanza d'Ercole)

74   G. B. ZELOTTI: *Venus* (central zone of the eastern wall in the Stanza di Venere)

75   G. B. ZELOTTI: frescoes on the western wall in the Stanza di Venere

76   G. B. ZELOTTI: *Venus Finding the Body of Adonis* (left-hand zone of the western wall in the Stanza di Venere)

77   G. B. ZELOTTI: *Venus Attempting to Seduce Adonis* (right-hand zone of the western wall in the Stanza di Venere)

78   G. B. ZELOTTI: *St. Jerome* (overdoor on the southern wall in the Stanza di Venere)

79   G. B. ZELOTTI: frescoes on the northern wall in the Stanza delle Arti

80   G. B. ZELOTTI: *Summer* (overdoor on the eastern wall in the Stanza delle Arti)

81   G. B. ZELOTTI: *Winter* (western wall in the Stanza delle Arti)

82   G. B. ZELOTTI: *Allegory of Music* (eastern wall in the Stanza delle Arti)

83   G. B. ZELOTTI: *Allegory of Sculpture* (eastern wall in the Stanza delle Arti)

84   G. B. ZELOTTI: *Allegory of Poetry* (southern wall in the Stanza delle Arti)

85   G. B. ZELOTTI: *Allegory of Painting* (southern wall in the Stanza delle Arti)

86   G. B. ZELOTTI: *Allegory of Astronomy* (left-hand zone of the northern wall in the Stanza delle Arti)

87   G. B. ZELOTTI: *Allegory of Architecture* (right-hand zone of the northern wall in the Stanza delle Arti)

88   G. B. ZELOTTI: *Holy Family* (overdoor on the northern wall in the Stanza delle Arti)

COLOR PLATES

SCALE DRAWINGS

SCALE DRAWINGS EXECUTED BY MARIO ZOCCONI AND ANDRZEJ PERESWIET SOŁTAN

PLATES

PLATES

1 - Villa Emo and the countryside around Fanzolo (Treviso). Aerial view

2 - Villa Emo: aerial view from the west

3 - Villa Emo: aerial view from the south

4 - Villa Emo: gene

of the south façade

5 - Villa Emo: three-quarter view from the western part of the garden

6 - Villa Emo: three-quarter view from the eastern part of the garden

7 - Villa Emo: southwest corner of the main block, showing the connection between it and the western wing

8 - Villa Emo: three-quarter view from the western lawn

9 - Villa Emo: façade of the main block

10 - Villa Emo: close-up view of the main block

11 - Villa Emo: junction between the corner column of the loggia and the western section of the façade

12 - Villa Emo: the two central columns of the loggia

13 - Villa Emo: bases of the loggia columns seen from the exterior

14 - Villa Emo: bases of the loggia columns seen from within

15 - Villa Emo: the tympanum sculptures

16 - Villa Emo: right-hand angle of the pediment and junction between the column and wall

17 - Villa Emo: connection of the column with the loggia wall

18 - Villa Emo: coffered ceiling of the loggia

19 - Villa Emo: gallery connecting the two wings

20 - Villa Emo: space underneath the loggia

21 - Villa Emo: passage under the ramp

22 - Villa Emo: western *barchessa* seen from the passage under the ramp

23 - Villa Emo: western *barchessa* seen from the incline of the ramp

24 - Villa Emo: western *barchessa* seen from within

25 - Villa Emo: eastern *barchessa*

26 - Villa Emo: end of the eastern *barchessa* with the dovecote

27 - Villa Emo: last two arches and dovecote of the western *barchessa*

28 - Villa Emo: arch of the western *barchessa*, with the chapel door in the rear wall

29 - Villa Emo: overall view of the north front of the main block and the *barchesse*

30 - Villa Emo: three-quarter view of the complex from the northwest

31 - Villa Emo: three-quarter view of the complex from the northeast

32 - Villa Emo: close-up corner view of the main block, the western *barchessa*, and dovecote, seen from the west

33 - Villa Emo: dovecote in the western *barchessa*

34 - Villa Emo: staircase connecting the successive floors of the main block

35 - Villa Emo: rear wall of the loggia

36 - G.B. Zelotti: figure of Ceres above the entrance portal of the loggia

37 - Villa Emo: western wall of the loggia (see fig. 39)

38 - Villa Emo: eastern wall of the loggia (see fig. 40)

39 - G. B. ZELOTTI: *Callisto Seduced by Jupiter Disguised as Diana* (western wall of the loggia)

40 - G. B. Zelotti: *Callisto Punished by Juno* (eastern wall of the loggia)

41 - G. B. Zelotti: *Allegory of Conjugal Love* (vestibule)

42 - G. B. Zelotti: *Allegory of Household Economy* (vestibule)

43 - G. B. ZELOTTI: *Grape-arbor with a Putto* (vestibule ceiling)

44 - Villa Emo: access arch from the vestibule into the central hall

45 - Villa Emo: northern end of the central hall, with the carved arms of the Emo family in the center

46 - Villa Emo: entrance arch into the central hall, with decorations by G. B. Zelotti

47 - Villa Emo: southern end of the central hall viewed from the left

48 - Villa Emo: southern end of the central hall viewed from the right

49 - G. B. ZELOTTI: frescoes on the western side of the central hall

50 - G. B. ZELOTTI: *The Continence of Scipio* (middle zone, western side of the central hall)

51 - G. B. Zᴇʟᴏᴛᴛɪ: frescoes on the eastern side of the central hall

52 - G. B. Zelotti: *The Death of Virginia* (middle zone, eastern side of the central hall)

53 - G. B. ZELOTTI: *Jupiter*, with a *Prisoner* beneath (left-hand zone, eastern side of the central hall)

54 - G. B. ZELOTTI: *Juno*, with a *Prisoner* beneath (right-hand zone, eastern side of the central hall)

55 - G. B. Zelotti: *Neptune*, with a *Prisoner* beneath (left-hand zone, western side of the central hall)

56 - G. B. ZELOTTI: *Cybele*, with a *Prisoner* beneath (right-hand zone, western side of the central hall)

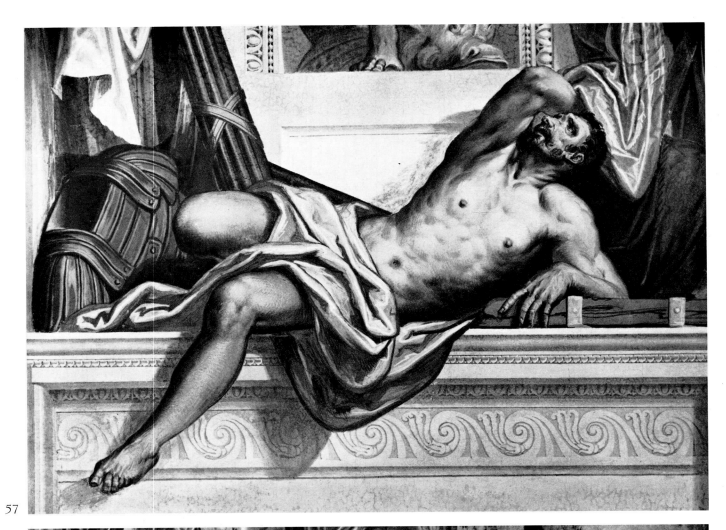

57

58

57 - G. B. ZELOTTI: *Prisoner beneath Neptune's Niche* (left-hand zone, western side of the central hall)
58 - G. B. ZELOTTI: *Prisoner beneath Cybele's Niche* (right-hand zone, western side of the central hall)

59 - Villa Emo: overall view of the central hall; south wall on the right, east on the left

60 - G. B. ZELOTTI: *Prudence* (over the entrance arch of the central hall)

61 - G. B. ZELOTTI: *Abundance* (over the entrance arch of the central hall)

62 - G. B. Zelotti: *Apollo and Daphne* (within panel); below, *Bust of Marcus Aurelius*
(flanking the entrance arch of the central hall)

63 - G. B. Zelotti: *The Contest of Apollo and Marsyas* (within panel); below, *Bust of Julius Caesar* (flanking the entrance arch of the central hall)

64

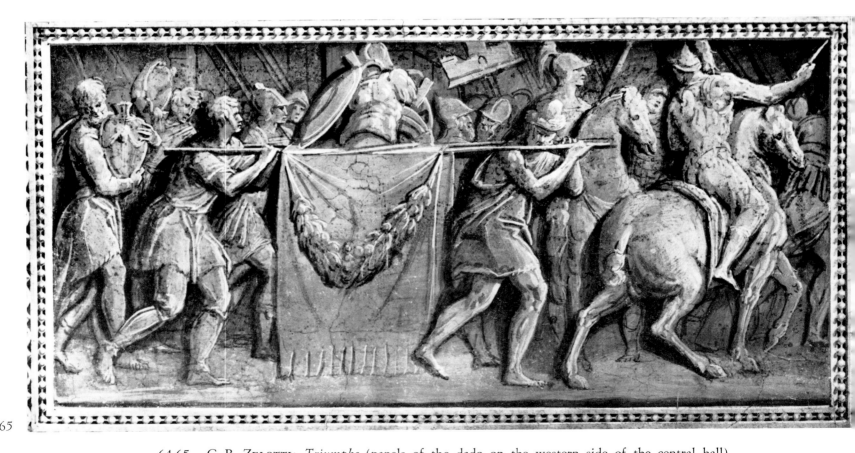

65

64-65 - G. B. ZELOTTI: *Triumphs* (panels of the dado on the western side of the central hall)

66

67

66-67 - G. B. Zelotti: *Triumphs* (panels of the dado on the eastern side of the central hall)

68 - G. B. Zᴇʟᴏᴛᴛɪ: *Hercules on the Pyre* (western wall in the Stanza d'Ercole)

69 - G. B. ZELOTTI: frescoes on the eastern wall in the Stanza d'Ercole

70 - G. B. Zelotti: *Hercules and Deianeira before the Body of Nessus*
(left-hand zone of the eastern wall in the Stanza d'Ercole)

71 - G. B. ZELOTTI: *Hercules Preparing to Throw Lichas into the Sea*
(right-hand zone of the eastern wall in the Stanza d'Ercole)

72 - G. B. Zelotti: *Fame* (overdoor on the eastern wall in the Stanza d'Ercole)

73 - G. B. Zelotti: *Noli me tangere* (overdoor on the southern wall in the Stanza d'Ercole)

74 - G. B. ZELOTTI: *Venus* (central zone of the eastern wall in the Stanza di Venere)

75 - G. B. Zelotti: frescoes on the western wall in the Stanza di Venere

76 - G. B. Zelotti: *Venus Finding the Body of Adonis* (left-hand zone of the western wall in the Stanza di Venere)

77 - G. B. Zelotti: *Venus Attempting to Seduce Adonis* (right-hand zone of the western wall in the Stanza di Venere)

78 - G. B. ZELOTTI: *St. Jerome* (overdoor on the southern wall in the Stanza di Venere)

79 - G. B. Zelotti: frescoes on the northern wall in the Stanza delle Arti

80 - G. B. ZELOTTI: *Summer* (overdoor on the eastern wall in the Stanza delle Arti)

81 - G.B. ZELOTTI: *Winter* (western wall in the Stanza delle Arti)

82 - G. B. ZELOTTI: *Allegory of Music* (eastern wall in the Stanza delle Arti)

83 - G. B. ZELOTTI: *Allegory of Sculpture* (eastern wall in the Stanza delle Arti)

84 - G. B. ZELOTTI: *Allegory of Poetry* (southern wall in the Stanza delle Arti)

85 - G. B. Zelotti: *Allegory of Painting* (southern wall in the Stanza delle Arti)

86 - G. B. ZELOTTI: *Allegory of Astronomy* (left-hand zone of the northern wall in the Stanza delle Arti)

87 - G. B. ZELOTTI: *Allegory of Architecture* (right-hand zone of the northern wall in the Stanza delle Arti)

88 - G. B. ZELOTTI: *Holy Family* (overdoor on the northern wall in the Stanza delle Arti)

89 - G. B. ZELOTTI: lunette above the window on the southern wall in the Stanza delle Arti

90

91

90-93 - G. B. ZELOTTI: four sections of the frieze beneath the cornice in the Stanza delle Arti

94 - G. B. Zelotti: frescoes on the northern wall in the Stanza di Io

95 - G. B. ZELOTTI: *Allegory of Spring* (eastern wall in the Stanza di Io)

96 - G. B. ZELOTTI: *Allegory of Autumn* (overdoor on the western wall in the Stanza di Io)

97 - G. B. ZELOTTI: *Ecce Homo* (overdoor on the northern wall in the Stanza di Io)

98 - G. B. ZELOTTI: *Juno Consigning Io to Argus* (left-hand zone on the southern wall in the Stanza di Io)

99 - G. B. ZELOTTI: *Mercury Charming Argus to Sleep* (right-hand zone on the southern wall in the Stanza di Io)

100 - G. B. Zelotti: *Mercury Beheading Argus* (left-hand zone on the western wall in the Stanza di Io)

101 - G. B. ZELOTTI: *Juno Discovering Argus* (right-hand zone on the western wall in the Stanza di Io)

102 - G. B. ZELOTTI: *Jupiter Seducing Io* (left-hand zone on the northern wall in the Stanza di Io)

103 - G.B. ZELOTTI: *Jupiter Transforming Io into a Heifer* (right-hand zone on the northern wall in the Stanza di Io)

104

105

106

107

104-107 - G. B. ZELOTTI: four sections of the frieze beneath the cornice in the Stanza di Io

108 - G. B. ZELOTTI: *Allegory of Fire, or Prophetic Divination* (wsetern chamber of grotesques, north wall)

109 - G. B. ZELOTTI: *Allegory of Pan, or Air* (western chamber of grotesques, north wall)

110 - G. B. Zelotti: *Allegories of the Balance and of Air, or Pan*
(western chamber of grotesques, east and north walls)

111 - G. B. ZELOTTI: *Allegory of Fire, or Prophetic Divination* (western chamber of grotesques, south wall)

112 - G. B. Zelotti: *Allegory of Pan, or Air* (western chamber of grotesques, south wall)

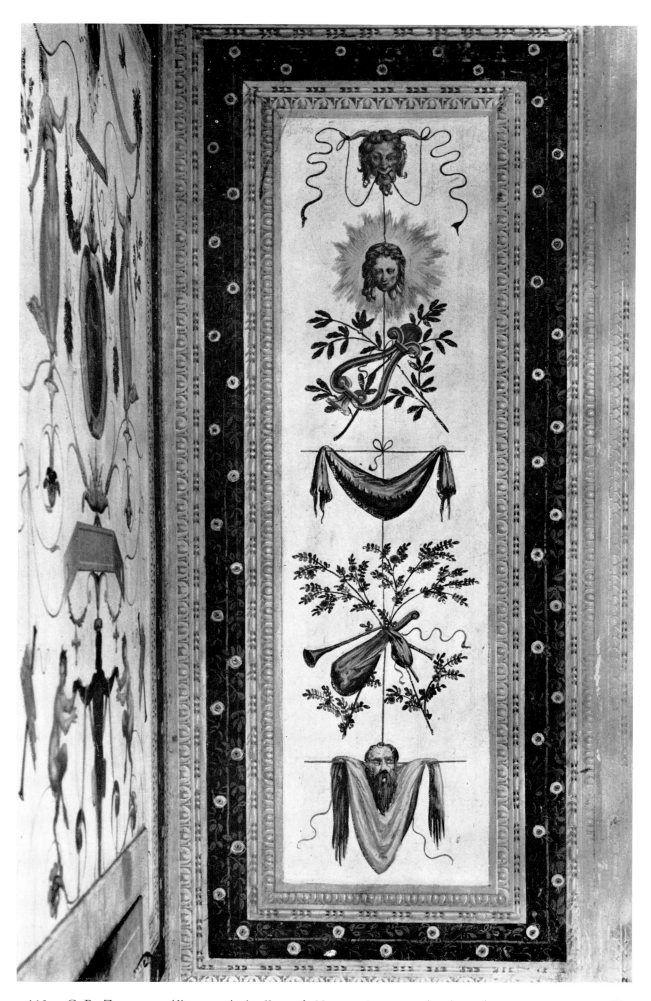

113 - G. B. Zelotti: *Allegory of Apollo and Marsyas* (western chamber of grotesques, west wall)

114 - G. B. ZELOTTI: *Allegories of the Balance and of Earth* (eastern chamber of grotesques, west and north walls)

115 - G. B. ZELOTTI: *Allegory of the Balance* (eastern chamber of grotesques, west wall)

116 - G. B. ZELOTTI: *Allegory of Earth* (eastern chamber of grotesques, north wall)

117 - G. B. Zelotti: detail of Persephone, in the *Allegory of Earth* (eastern chamber of grotesques, north wall)

118 - G. B. Zelotti: *Allegory of Earth* (eastern chamber of grotesques, south wall)

119 - G. B. ZELOTTI: detail of a satyr, in the *Allegory of the Balance* (eastern chamber of grotesques, west wall)

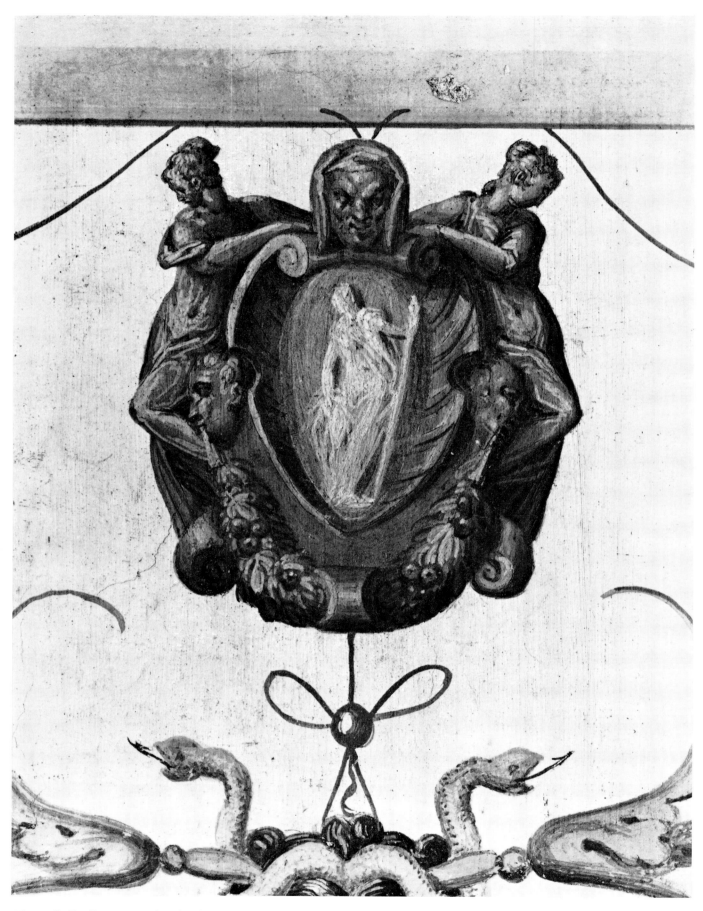

120 - G. B. ZELOTTI: detail of the *Allegory of Water, or Amphitrite* (eastern chamber of grotesques, south wall)

121 - G. B. ZELOTTI: *Medusa*—detail of the *Allegory of Water, or Amphitrite*
(eastern chamber of grotesques, south wall)

SCALE DRAWINGS

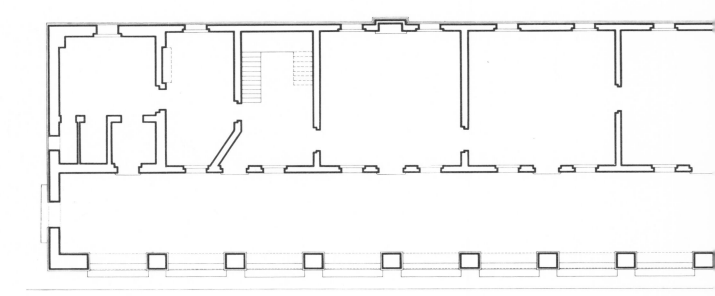

b - Villa Emo: plan of the ground floor

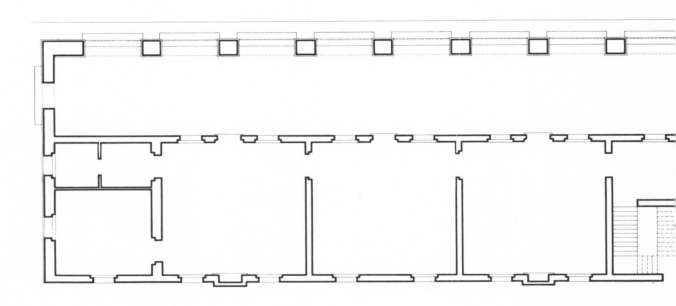

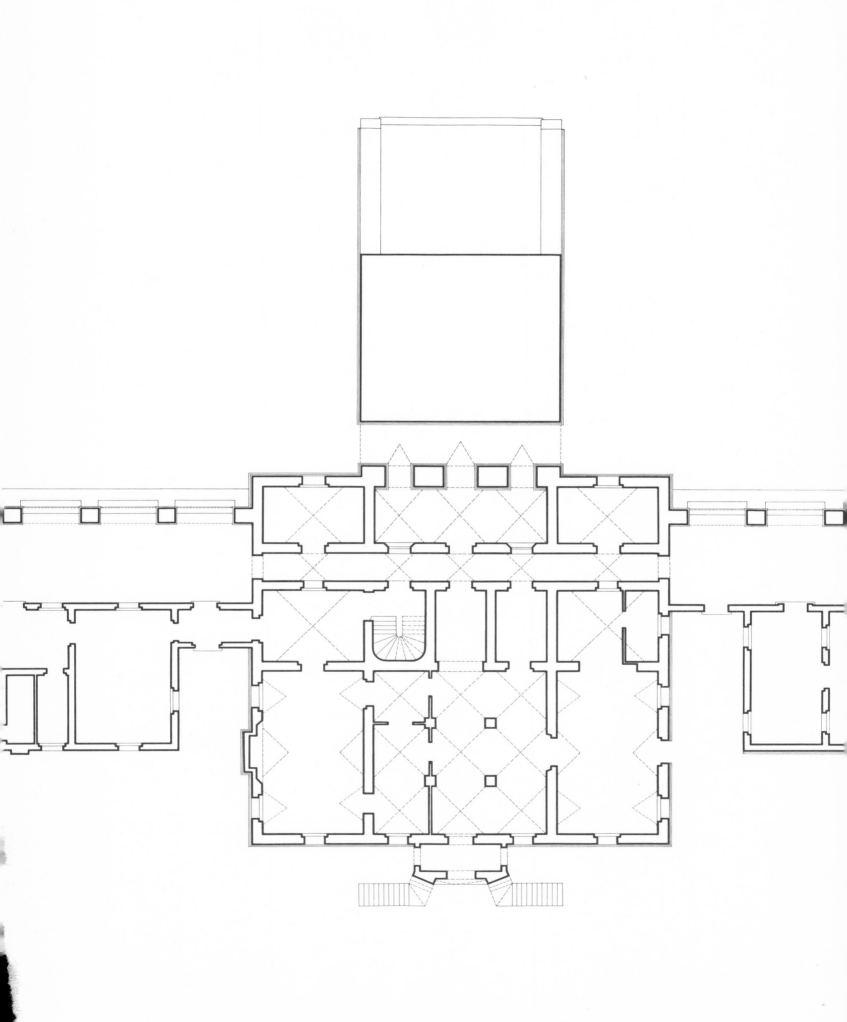

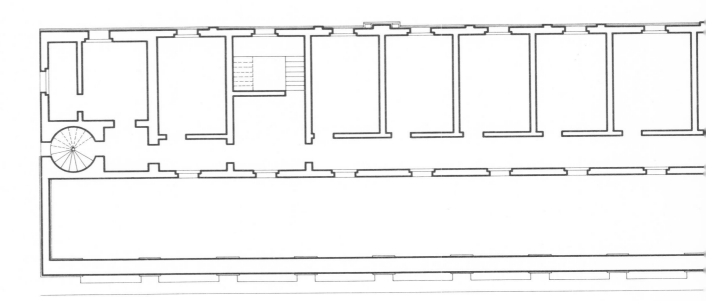

c - Villa Emo: plan of the main floor (central block) and connecting upper floor of the wings

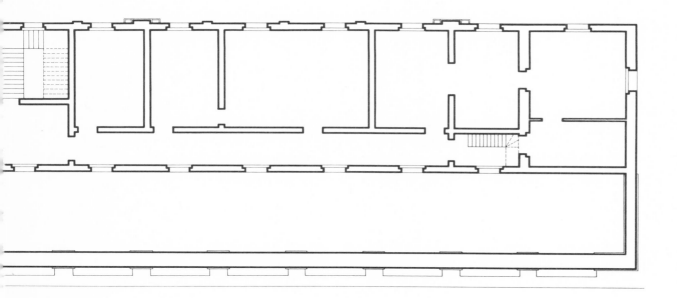

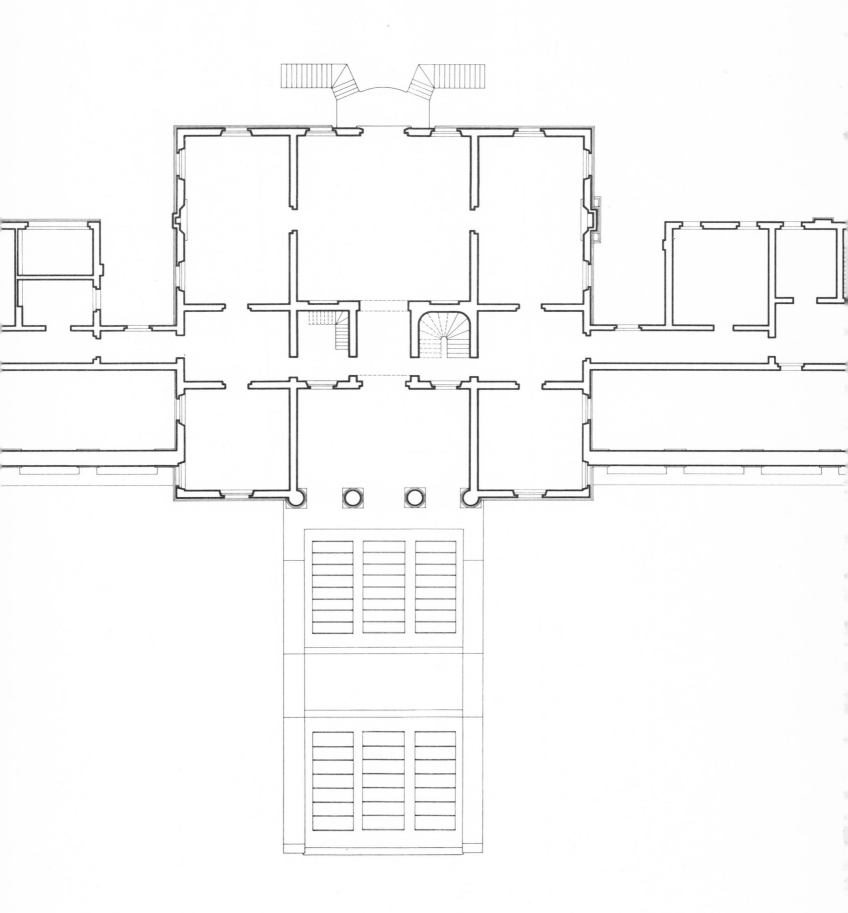

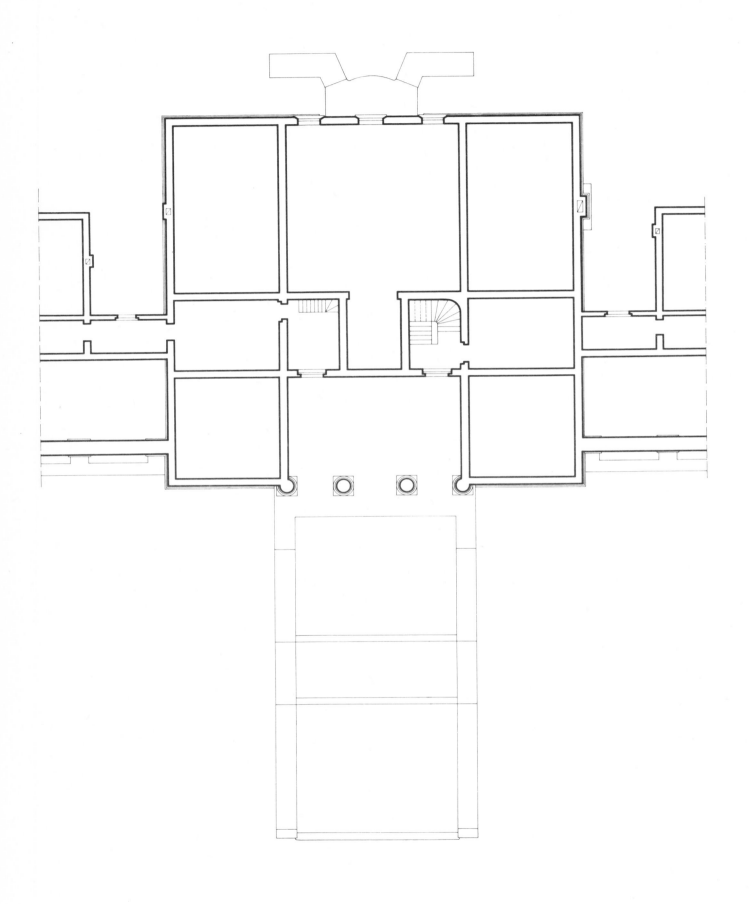

d - Villa Emo: plan of the mezzanine level (central block)

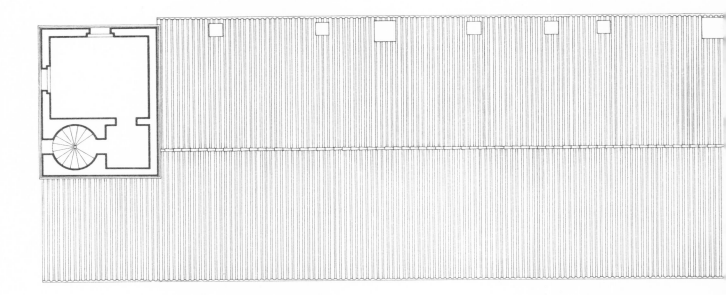

e - Villa Emo: attic plan of the central block and dovecotes

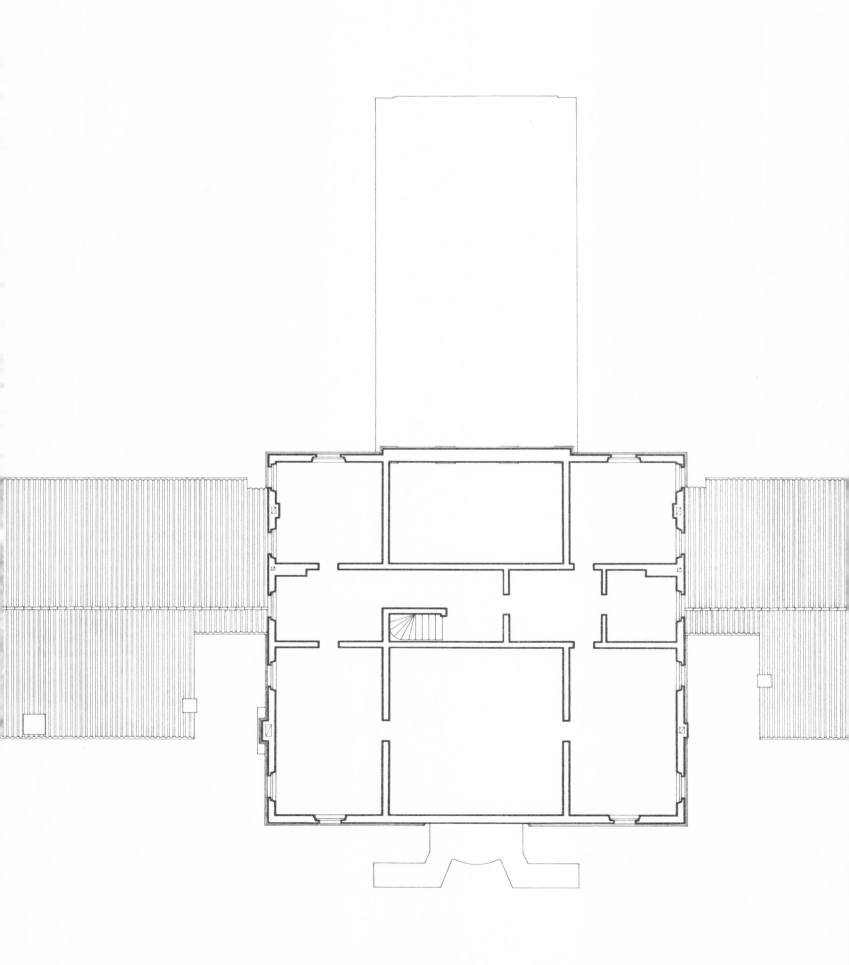

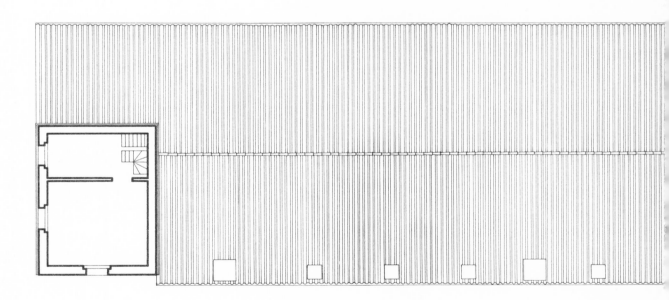

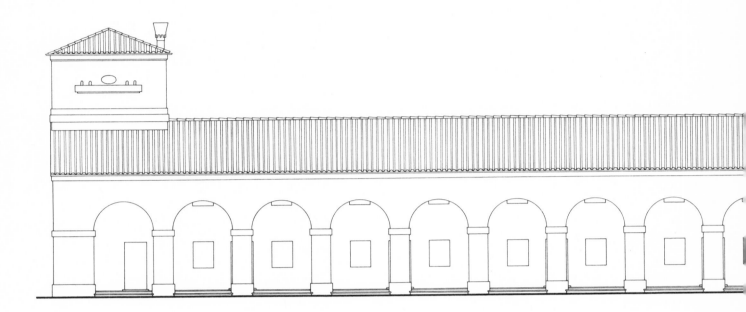

f - Villa Emo: front elevation

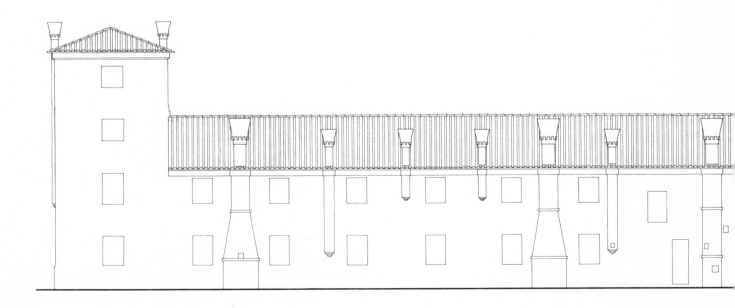

g - Villa Emo: rear elevation

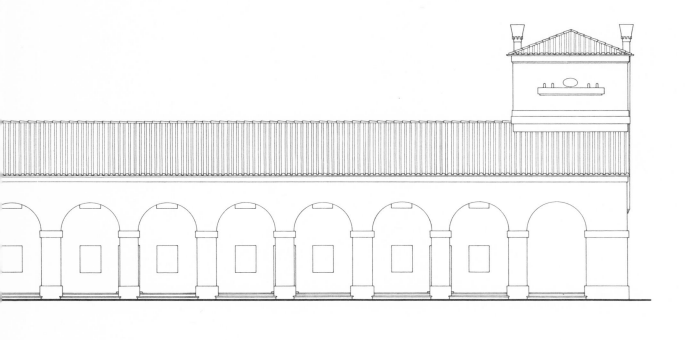

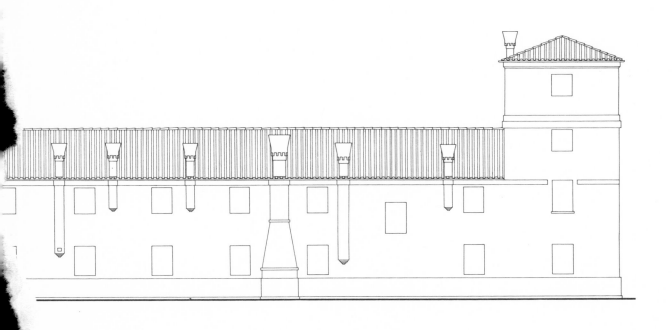

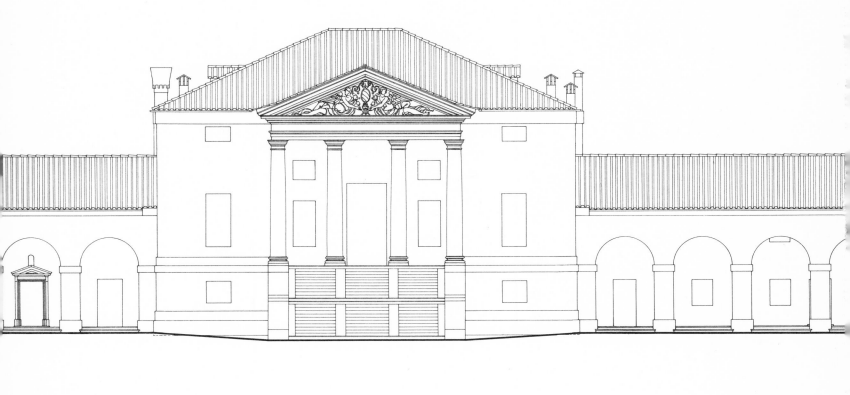

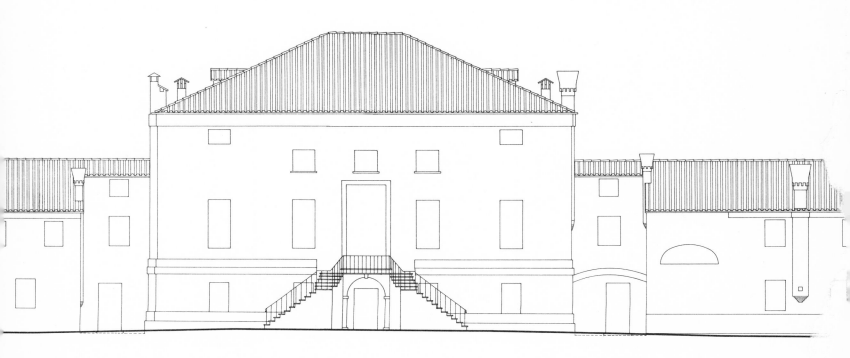

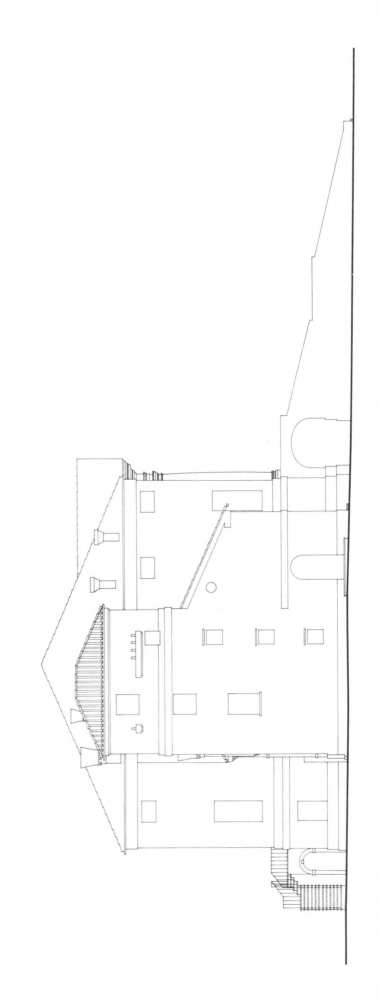

b - Villa Emo: elevation of the west side

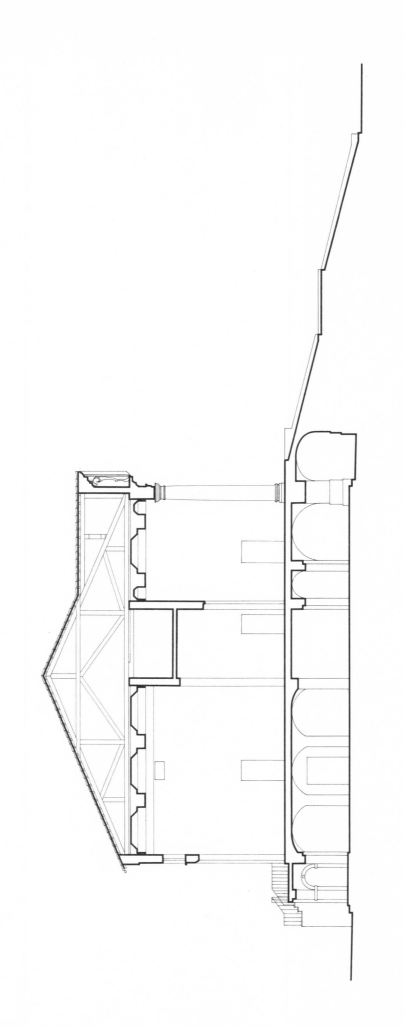

i - Villa Emo: transverse section of the central block

0 1m   5   10   15m

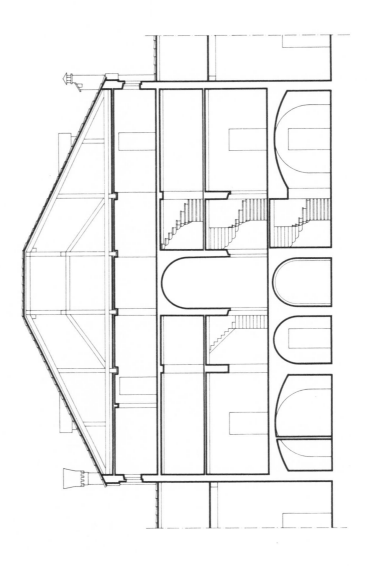

j - Villa Emo: longitudinal section of the central block

0   1m   5   10   15m

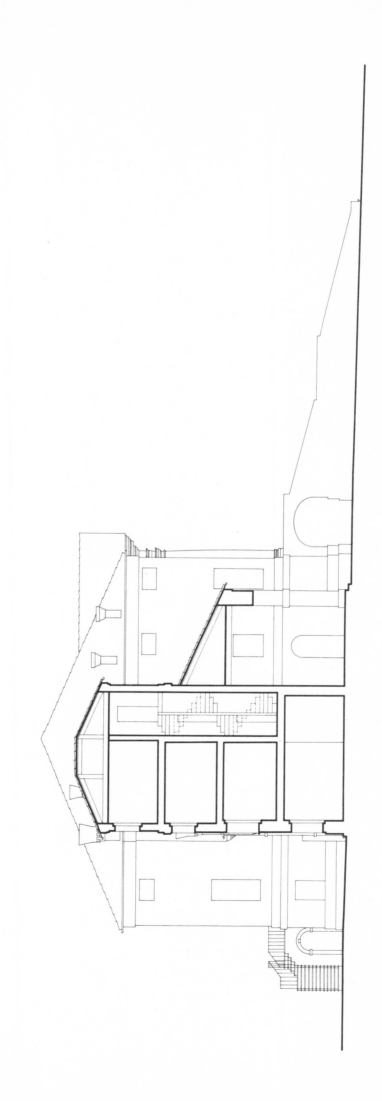

k - Villa Emo: transverse section of the dovecote and portico, with the western flank of the central block

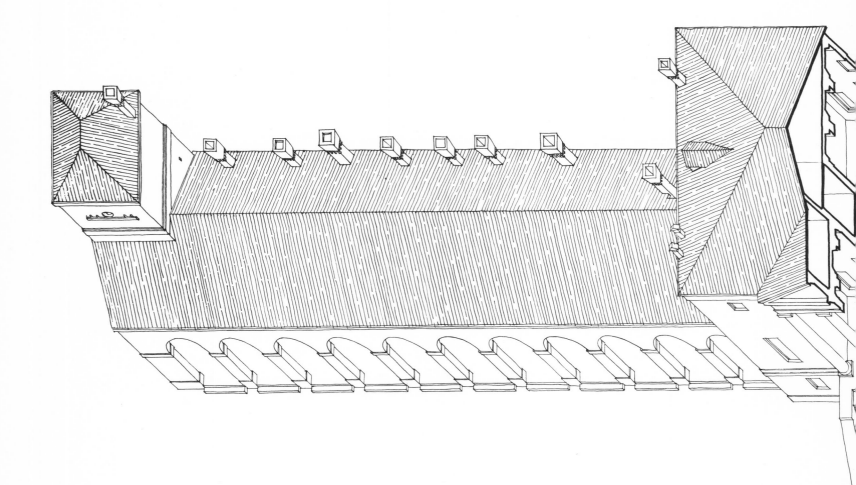

l - Villa Emo: axonometric view

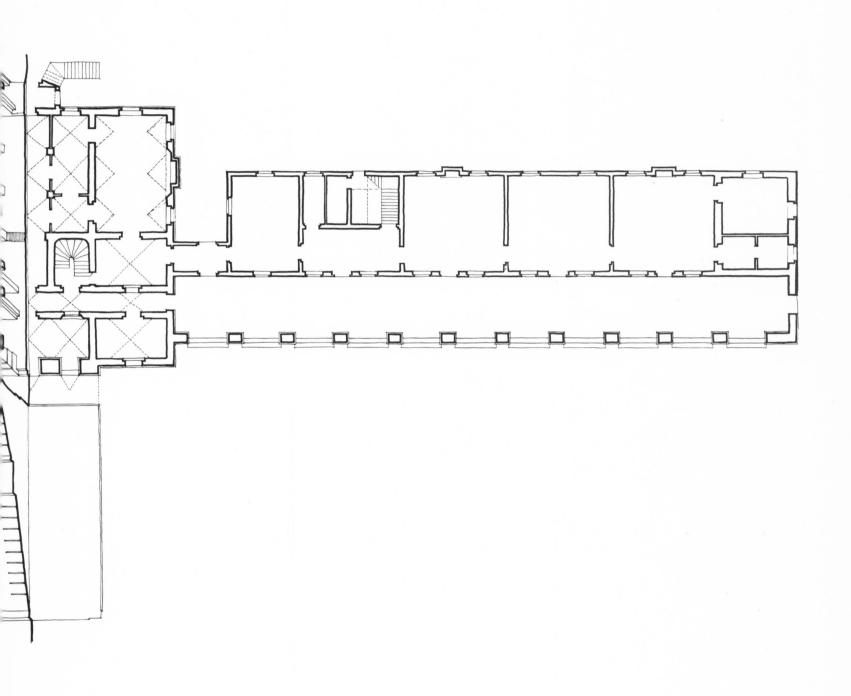

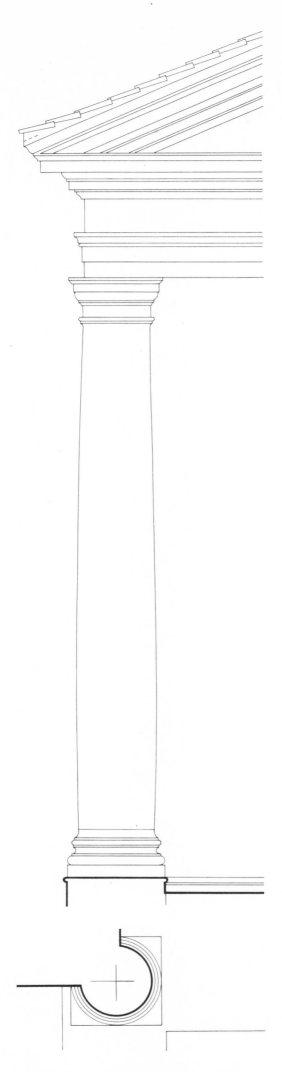

m - Villa Emo: detail of the order

0   0,5   1m   2   3m